Small Space Garden Ideas

Small Space
Garden Ideas

Philippa Pearson

DK

LONDON, NEW YORK, MUNICH, MELBOURNE, DELHI

Editor Holly Kyte
Project Art Editor Vicky Read
Senior Editor Alastair Laing
Senior Designer Sonia Moore
Pre-production Producer Rebecca Fallowfield
Senior Producer Alex Bell
Jacket Designer Rosie Levine
Senior Jacket Creative Nicola Powling
Managing Editor Penny Warren
Art Director Jane Bull
Publisher Mary Ling

DK Publishing
Editor Kate Johnsen
North American Consultant Lori Spencer
Senior Editor Shannon Beatty

Project Photography Will Heap,
Debbie Patterson, Andy Crawford
Illustrations Bryony Fripp

This edition first published in 2014 by DK Publishing,
4th floor, 345 Hudson Street, New York, New York 10014

Copyright © 2014 Dorling Kindersley Limited
15 16 17 18 19 10 9 8 7 6 5 4 3 2 1
001—196653—Feb/2014

Published in Great Britain by Dorling Kindersley Limited.

A catalog record for this book is available from the
Library of Congress.

ISBN 978-1-4654-1586-8

DK books are available at special discounts when purchased in
bulk for sales promotions, premiums, fund-raising, or educational
use. For details, contact: DK Publishing Special Markets, 345 Hudson
Street, New York, New York 10014 or SpecialSales@dk.com.

Color reproduction by Altaimage UK
Printed and bound by South China Printing Co. Ltd. China

Discover more at
www.dk.com

Contents

SMALL SPACE,
BIG POTENTIAL

Maximizing Your Space

Even if your gardening space is tiny to nonexistent, you can still fill it with greenery and bring plants into your life. We've created over 40 inspiring and fun gardening projects that will add color, interest, and a "wow!" factor to your home, whether you have the tiniest courtyard, a balcony, or just an outside step.

Grow in Miniature

Small is beautiful, so think big and put eye-catching plants in unusual and interesting containers. You'll be surprised at what will grow in a teacup, tin can, or kitchen utensil—all great sizes for placing on tables, windowsills, steps, and ledges for a miniature gardening world to enjoy inside and out.

Terrariums are miniature gardens enclosed in glass and designed to be easy to look after.

Create a tiny barnyard garden in a cake pan. Fun for the whole family!

Garden in the Air

Look up! The space above your head doesn't need to be bare, it can be transformed into a hanging garden. With the right plants and innovative airborne containers, you can plant ceilings, walls, railings, porches, and window frames with a whole range of flowering and edible plants, so that even the tiniest balcony or entrance porch can be blooming.

Kokedama is the Japanese art of hanging plants in moss balls tied with string.

TOPSY-TURVY
Make use of limited space and grow plants in lampshades for a fun feature. These chile peppers thrive on being planted upside down.

Air plants are perfect for growing in hanging arrangements because they don't need soil to live.

Take the Vertical Challenge

If your only space is vertical, climbing plants don't need to be your only option. Get creative and upcycle your upward space with unusual vertical planters, such as picture frames and stepladders. With the right planter, your vertical space can be opened up to all sorts of different plants.

Gutters and old picture frames make good use of vertical space, while wine boxes can be turned into a miniature greenhouse.

Customize Your Containers

Make the most of terra-cotta pots by painting them in bright colors and decorating with prints and patterns. Or try making your own containers: drill a few drainage holes and all sorts of charming vintage objects can be used for growing plants; while wooden boxes can be given a contemporary makeover by covering them with slate.

You'll be surprised how easy it is to create your own stylish and contemporary planters out of simple concrete—give it a try!

Transform terra-cotta pots with paint and decoupage decoration.

PERSONALIZE POTS

With a little creativity, an ordinary pot can be turned into a stunning and useful container for showing off your favorite plants.

Gardening in a small space shouldn't restrict your ideas or planting opportunities. Accept the challenge and discover new possibilities!

◄━ High Impact Planting

You may be surprised by the sheer range of plants it's possible to grow in small spaces. Enjoy your plants to the max by choosing ones with interesting flowers, scent, foliage, architectural shapes, or edible elements.

Bonsai, herbs, planting for wildlife, fruit, succulents, and carnivorous plants can easily be grown in small spaces.

Play Host to Wildlife

By selecting the right plants and creating habitats, even the smallest garden patch can become a special place for wildlife, attracting insects like bees, butterflies, and ladybugs that will also help you out by pollinating and keeping pests in check. And happily, insects seem to share our love of brightly colored flowers!

Make a pretty insect hotel for friendly creatures to hibernate in, with a roof space for plants as well.

A wildflower meadow is surprisingly well suited to growing in an old drawer, while you can both feed the birds and feast your eyes with these decorative bird stations.

Practical Checklist

Before you start to plant up your gardening space, get started with the right tools and equipment (see pages 244–5), and take time to learn about different plants and their needs (see pages 224–43). Consider how much time you can allocate to looking after your plants; jobs like watering, feeding, and pruning. Here are some essential pointers to help you get started.

CONTAINERS

- Choose a container that is big enough for plant growth and repot plants when roots get bigger.
- Make sure there are drainage holes in the container and add some if there aren't.
- Add extra drainage like gravel or crocks to the bottom of containers.
- Consider frost-proof containers for exposed sites.

WATERING AND FEEDING

- Containers can dry out quickly in warm, sunny, and exposed sites and, unless you choose drought-tolerant plants, will need watering frequently, sometimes twice a day.
- Try to ensure easy access to water, or work out a strategy that will lessen the burden of watering.
- Put saucers under containers to protect surfaces and retain moisture.
- Most plants generally need regular watering and feeding in their growing season, but won't need any when they are dormant, usually in winter.

RIGHT PLANT, RIGHT PLACE

- Assess the growing conditions in your garden space before planting. Does it get a lot of sun? Does it get wet when it rains or is it sheltered? Is it in a windy location?
- Once you know the growing conditions of your site, choose plants that will survive and thrive in these conditions; a plant that loves the sun, for example, may not grow well in the shade.
- Planting high up in an exposed location where it is dry and windy, such as on a balcony, will need plants that are suited to these conditions.

KEEP THINGS SMALL

- Watch for plants that are grown especially for smaller spaces, such as dwarf types of larger plants like fruit trees.
- With regular pruning, however, many larger plants can be kept in check and maintain a compact size better suited to a small site.

Choose the right plants and containers, then just add your creativity for fabulous small space gardening.

STORAGE FEATURE
Make a feature out of storing garden tools by upcycling a storage chest or cupboard. Simply decorate with exterior paint and place a planted container on top.

MICRO GARDEN

TOOLS & EQUIPMENT

cake pans in several sizes
(make sure they are not
the loose-bottomed variety)

clear-drying superglue

thick, clear acetate

scissors

spoon

small gravel and sand in several
different colors and grades

florist's ornamental Spanish moss
(optional)

pencil

Velcro adhesive pads

PLANT LIST

selection of small air plants:
Tillandsia bulbosa
Tillandsia caput medusae
Tillandsia ionantha
Tillandsia pruniosa
Tillandsia streptophylla

Vertically Mounted

Air Plant Canisters

Great fun and simple to make, these planted canisters look like miniature desert landscapes and provide a novel means of decorating a wall, fence, or even your front door with some quirky living greenery.

 TIME IT RIGHT Late spring or summer is a good time to plant your canisters since air plants aren't frost hardy. Put the canisters outside for summer, bringing them indoors from mid-fall.

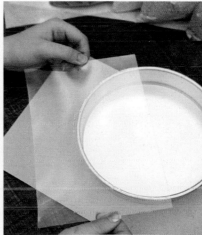

1 Apply a small amount of superglue around one half of the outside rim of a cake pan. Be careful not to apply too much.

2 Press a rectangle of acetate over the glued half of the rim so that it covers it completely with sufficient overlap.

Project Steps

3 Leave to dry completely overnight, then neatly cut around the cake pan rim with a pair of scissors to remove the excess acetate.

4 Spoon layers of sand and gravel into the "planting chamber"; this is for decorative purposes—air plants don't need soil to grow. Build up contrasting layers until the plants will be able to set comfortably and longer leaves can extend over the rim of the acetate. Top with florist's ornamental moss for extra decoration, if you like.

5 Select your air plants, choosing different shapes, colors, and leaf textures for interest. Don't overfill the pans; the smallest pans work best with a single bold plant, while two or more plants in larger pans look better if plants contrast in style or have similar qualities that work well as a group.

6 Position the air plants so that they are stable and evenly spaced. Hold the cake pans up to the wall or fence and create an arrangement that works for you. With a pencil, mark where the tops of each pan will be positioned.

7 Stick half a Velcro pad near the top of each pan, then stick the other half at the matching point on the wall or fence, ensuring all pads are level. Press the pans on to the wall so that the pads are exactly aligned.

Care Advice

Where to site
Air plants like warmth but not direct sunlight and are happy outdoors from spring to early fall. Bring inside before temperatures drop below 46°F (8°C). Keep plants indoors where light levels and air circulation are good. Do not place near heat sources; a damp atmosphere is preferable.

Watering
Air plants absorb moisture through their leaves and should be sprayed 2–3 times a week (ideally with rainwater), more frequently during summer or in dry conditions. Give plants a soak at least once a month by submerging them in room temperature water for a little while, but be sure to shake off any excess water.

General care
Remove any dead, diseased, or dying foliage and do not to let any water sit in the base of the plant because this could cause it to rot.

Feed with a diluted special air plant liquid fertilizer misted on leaves once a week in spring and summer, every two weeks in winter.

TOOLS & EQUIPMENT

collection of tin cans with appealing
  designs printed onto the metal

masking tape

electric drill & drill bits

gravel

soil-based potting mix

horticultural grit

small scoop or spoon

dibber, chopstick, or pencil

decorative gravel

PLANT LIST

Aloe aristata

Aloe brevifolia

Chamaelobivia kawinai

Chamaelobivia 'Rose Quartz'

Echeveria agavoides 'Red Edge'

Haworthia glauca var. *herrei*
  f. *jacobseniana*

Pachyphytum hookerii

Rebutia species

Sedum 'Spiral Staircase'

Stenocereus dumortieri

Mexican-style

Tin Can Cacti Planters

For a taste of Mexico without leaving your garden, create a desert scene with architectural cacti and juicy succulents grouped together in bright food cans for an interesting table display.

TIME IT RIGHT Best to plant at the start of the growing season from mid-spring. Plants will last 1–3 years before needing to be repotted, depending on the size of the plant and can.

1 Clean the tin cans thoroughly before using. Drill drainage holes in the bottom of each can with an electric drill. Use masking tape to keep the drill from slipping.

2 Add a layer of drainage material, such as gravel, to the bottom of each can. Good drainage is vital so that the roots don't sit in water and rot.

4 Place plants on a layer of compost and then fill in around the root ball, working in the compost with a dibber to reduce air pockets. Tap the container on the work surface to distribute the compost evenly. Top with a layer of decorative gravel. Place on a saucer or small plate if you need to protect the table surface.

3 Mix up a free-draining gritty compost from soil-based potting mix and horticultural grit in 3:1 proportions. Remove plants from their pots and gently break up the root ball, teasing out the roots and removing soil. Be careful not to damage the roots.

Care Advice

Where to site Cacti and succulents need a sunny site and warmth to thrive. You can leave them outside in summer, as long as there is adequate protection and shelter from rain. Bring inside during winter and place on a sunny windowsill in a warm room.

Watering and feeding The easiest way to water these is to place the cans in a shallow container of water, leave until the surface of the compost is moist, then lift out and allow to drain. Water regularly in the growing season—every 10 days or so—and add a diluted liquid feed to the water during spring and summer. Do not feed or water in fall and winter.

Repot plants into large containers when roots start to show through the can's drainage hole. Repotting is best done in spring, and watering plants a couple of days before keeps roots moist.

Create a dramatic scene by matching the shape of plants to the design and size of the cans

TOOLS & EQUIPMENT

large glass lantern with opening

electric drill & drill bits (optional)

pond liner or similar

strong outdoor adhesive

strip of thick, clear plastic

2 contrasting types of gravel

soil-based potting mix mixed 3:1 with horticultural grit

dibber, chopstick, or pencil

PLANT LIST

Abromeitiella brevifolia

carpet moss (optional)

Crassula columella

Echeveria minima

Frithia pulchra

x *Pachyveria* 'Powder Puff'

Care Advice

General care Water every 10 days from spring to early fall by wetting the soil between plants with a water mister; include a diluted liquid feed. Leave the door open for air but bring inside over the winter.

Moroccan-style

Lantern Garden

A glass lantern is easily adapted to house a miniature display of succulents for a stylish centerpiece that works both indoors and out.

TIME IT RIGHT This project can be completed in an hour and is best started in spring or summer when the plants will be actively growing.

1 Drill drainage holes in the base of the lantern, if required, then insert pond liner. Glue the plastic strip across the bottom third of the open side. Add a layer of gravel followed by a layer of potting mix.

2 Arrange a selection of plants inside to suit the height and space of the lantern, then plant them with the help of a dibber. Cover the surface with gravel.

3 If you like, line the top rim too and plant with moss, but make sure the moss doesn't dry out.

Pots and Pots of

Gourmet Microgreens

Make your own mini windowsill propagators with plastic cups and their domed lids, perfect for growing a collection of tasty, nutritious microgreens in the smallest of spaces.

TOOLS & EQUIPMENT

plastic drink cups with domed lids

metal skewer or similar

garden twine

scissors

all-purpose adhesive

small package labels

soil-based potting mix

SEED LIST

beet 'Bull's Blood'

mustard green 'Osaka Purple'

Swiss chard 'Bright Lights'

lots of strong-tasting plants are
  suitable for growing as microgreens,
  others to try include:
    radishes; herbs such as basil,
    coriander, and fennel; other
    Chinese greens like mizuna;
    and even less exotic vegetables
    like broccoli and kale

 TIME IT RIGHT Seeds are best sown from early spring to early fall, when they will germinate quickly and you should be snipping leaves for salad in 1–2 weeks. Germination in winter willl be slower and more erratic.

1 Wash your drink cups and lids thoroughly, leave to dry, then assemble the ingredients to make your mini propagators.

Project Steps

2 Drainage is vital to prevent the seedlings from setting in too much water and rotting. Carefully pierce the base of each container a few times to create drainage holes.

3 Decorate each cup by tying bands of garden twine around the top and bottom, and add a package label on the top band. Glue the string in place at several points and leave for a couple of hours while the glue dries.

4 Fill the cups with seed potting mix, leaving a gap of 1¼–1½in (3–4cm) below the rim for watering.

5 Gently tap the whole cup on a hard surface to remove any air pockets that may prevent water from being distributed evenly through the soil. This also lets the potting mix settle and creates a nice, even growing surface for your seeds.

7 Sprinkle a thin layer of potting mix over the seeds—just enough to cover them—then water your pot, put the domed lid on top, and write the plant's name on the label. Place a container under the pot to prevent water from damaging surfaces and position on a sunny windowsill or outside in warmer weather.

6 Put some seeds in the cradle of your palm and lightly sprinkle them over the surface of the soil mix. You are aiming to create an even spread, so the seeds are sown closely, but are not clumped together.

Care Advice

Where to site and watering Place on a sunny windowsill in a warm room to aid germination. In warmer weather, you can leave the pots outside, but if frost is forecast, bring them inside. Do not overwater, especially in the early stages because this will prevent seed germination. Water pots regularly once shoots are growing, and frequently in warmer weather.

Harvesting You need to harvest quickly and regularly. The optimal harvest time ranges from 7–14 days after sowing, depending on the variety. Crop by snipping the small leaves with scissors just before you are ready to serve. If you need to harvest shoots earlier, place in a plastic bag with a little water and put in the refrigerator to keep fresh.

Take the lid off your pot once shoots are beginning to grow so plants have more air circulation and space to grow.

TOOLS & EQUIPMENT

colander with feet

card

pencil

scissors

hanging basket liner

multipurpose potting mix

large scoop or trowel

watering can

SEED LIST

Batavia leaf lettuce

Red leaf lettuce

Cut-and-come-again

Colorful Salad Colander

Sow red and green leaf lettuce seeds in a vintage colander for a stunning effect inspired by patchwork. It makes an impressive display at dinner parties where guests can cut their own fresh salad leaves.

TIME IT RIGHT Sow cut-and-come-again lettuce from spring to early fall and also through fall and into winter by using seasonal varieties. You should be cutting the first harvest in 4–5 weeks.

1 Place your colander upside down on some thick cardstock and draw around the rim. Then draw another circle inside the outline, ¾–1½in (2–4cm) smaller.

2 Within the smaller circle, draw your stencil design. Keep it simple; we divided the circle into four quadrants. Cut out your stencil, and keep all the shapes.

 Project Steps

3 Place a hanging-basket liner inside the colander—this will help to keep soil and moisture inside the container. Cut to shape, to just below the rim for a cleaner look.

4 Fill the colander with multipurpose potting mix to just under the level of the liner, then tap the colander down on a hard surface to get rid of any air pockets and to level the surface.

5 Water the soil surface well at this stage so as not to disperse the seeds in the design.

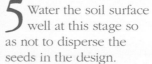

Care Advice

Watering You won't need to water for a few days to start with since you have watered the soil mix before sowing; it is then best to spray with a mister to stop seeds from dispersing before germination and disrupting the design. Make sure the soil mix doesn't dry out. Water overhead once seeds have germinated using a watering can with a fine nozzle, but do not overwater since the small seedlings may die off in too much moisture. In very dry summer conditions, place the colander in a container filled with water up to the level of the colander's base so that it absorbs water from underneath; this method will also stop seeds from dispersing before germination.

Feeding Use a light liquid feed between harvests to encourage more leaves to grow back for cutting.

Thin out after germination by lightly pulling seedlings from the soil mix. This increases air circulation and helps to keep the plants less congested and the design more structured.

6 Cover alternate sections of the design with stencils and sow lettuce seeds of one color, then cover the sown areas with stencils and sow the remaining areas with the other lettuce seeds.

7 Remove stencils and sprinkle a layer of soil mix over all the seeds to cover them lightly, then place in a warm, bright place, or outside in summer. Note that red lettuce seedlings will be green at first and then change to red as the plants mature.

More Salad Planting Ideas

Why not try growing lettuce in other containers? Wicker baskets are great because, like colanders, they allow drainage. Metal adds a vintage look, while for something quirky, cut the base off plastic milk jugs, plant them, and hang on a wall. Lettuces can be decorative; they're perfect to plant on the edges of beds and with other herbs and ornamental plants in containers.

As well as lettuce, you can grow plenty of edible flowers that will add a splash of color to your planting and an unusual zing to your salads, such as calendula (top center), nasturtiums, pansies, and primroses.

TOOLS & EQUIPMENT

clear glass container with lid or
   dome, such as a hurricane lamp,
   canning jar, bell cloche, or
   cake cover

gravel or small pebbles

small potting scoop or spoon

activated carbon granules

soil-based potting mix

dibber, chopstick, or pencil

bonsai or ordinary tweezers

water mister

PLANT LIST

carpet moss

Dionaea muscipula

Hosta 'Blue Mouse Ears'

Hosta 'Cracker Crumbs'

Hosta 'Iced Lemon'

Nepenthes x *ventrata*

Scleranthus uniflorus

Utricularia sandersonii

Closed Glass

Terrarium

A mini garden encased in glass, a terrarium makes an
eye-catching display and is the perfect choice if you
lack space and time for a real garden. It is easy to
look after, so even better if you lack a green thumb.

TIME IT RIGHT Plant in spring or summer
when plants are actively growing. Plants should last
2–3 years without needing to be transferred to a larger
container and can be kept smaller by pruning.

1 Choose a transparent container
and lid appropriate to the size
of your plants, with room for the
planting medium and growing.
Terrariums have no drainage holes
so, to keep roots from rotting, it is
vital to include a generous layer of
gravel to collect excess water.

2 Use a spoon to sprinkle a
thin layer of activated carbon
granules (available from aquatic
suppliers) over the gravel. This will
help to keep the container smelling
sweet by filtering out impurities.
Wash the carbon granules first to
remove any residue.

Project Steps

3 Next, add some planting medium. What you put in depends on the plants you choose, but a peat-like potting mix that retains moisture and allows drainage is a good choice. Add a layer of the potting mix and lightly pat down with a dibber, chopstick, or pencil.

PLANTING TIPS

Choose plants that will remain small and prefer low light and high humidity. Ferns, dwarf hostas, bog plants, carnivorous and tropical plants are good choices. Avoid succulents and cacti since they prefer a drier, sunnier environment.

4 Get your plants ready for planting by removing any loose soil and gently teasing any pot-bound roots. Make a small depression in the mix, then carefully position your plant in the soil.

5 Add more potting mix around the sides of the plant, gently tapping it into position with a dibber, chopstick, or pencil. Make sure that there is enough soil for roots to continue growing before going on to the next step.

6 Fill in around the plants with moss using tweezers. You can also add items from nature, such as twigs, driftwood, stones, pebbles, or shells to create a mini landscape scene in the terrarium.

7 Remove soil from the sides of the glass with a mister. Water then seal and leave the terrarium to create its own atmosphere. If the glass mists up inside, it is working!

Care Advice

Where to site
You must place your terrarium out of direct sunlight, so don't choose a sunny windowsill. The plants need low light, but enough to be able to grow without becoming straggly.

Watering
The key to a terrarium is that it is self-sufficient. Plants form condensation in the enclosed environment, water drips down the sides and they water themselves. If the condensation stops or the soil looks dry, water plants by using a meat baster or misting the inside. Don't overwater, especially in winter. Tropical or carnivorous plants need a bit more water, preferring rainwater, and while they do not enjoy being soggy they must always be wet, so maintain the water level at 2in (5cm) below the surface of the soil. Add more sand to the planting medium for these plants, too.

General care
Air the terrarium every 2–3 weeks for a few hours, especially in the spring and summer. If you've chosen the right plants and the right container size to match, the terrarium will keep going for a while without needing replacement plants. You can keep plants in shape by pruning; make sure you remove any trimmed foliage and any plant that begins to rot. Plants rot because of too much moisture, so you will need to correct the balance by opening the lid more frequently. The soil can be refreshed after some time by scraping off the surface and replacing it with fresh potting mix.

Terrariums were originally used
by Victorian plant hunters to
transport their living specimens
thousands of miles home

Instant Bonsai

Instant bonsai is all about creating a natural miniature landscape using moss and readily available plants. Delicate but bold, it makes a dynamic impact.

TIME IT RIGHT Early spring is the best time to pot your plant, not when the plant is dormant in winter. You can choose evergreen or deciduous sapling trees, shrubs, or perennials.

TOOLS & EQUIPMENT

akadama (baked clay particles)

keto (peat soil)

black lava rock particles

large bowl for mixing soils

bonsai or general-purpose fertilizer

container with drainage hole

plastic mesh

scissors

aluminum wire

wire cutters

tweezers

small pruners or bonsai scissors

small scoop

dibber, chopstick, or pencil

spatula

water mister

PLANT LIST

a compact moss, such as woodland or carpet types

Pinus thunbergii (Japanese Black Pine)

Akadama

Black lava rock particles

Keto

1 Select your soils first: 3 parts akadama, 1 part keto, 1 part black lava rock. These specialty soils meet the needs of smaller containers by absorbing and retaining moisture but also allowing excess water to drain.

2 Mix your soils with a little bonsai or general-purpose fertilizer. Make sure the pot you use has a drainage hole in the bottom; this is to prevent the roots from sitting in water and rotting.

Project Steps

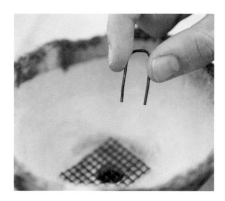

3 Cut out a square of mesh to size and position it over the drainage hole; this will stop the potting mix from falling through and prevent clogging, enabling vital airflow. Cut a short section of aluminum wire with wire cutters and bend it into a U-shape.

4 Insert the wire through the middle of the mesh. Make sure the wire ends come through the drainage hole, then bend them so that they are flush with the bottom of the bowl to fix the mesh in place.

5 Carefully take your plant out of its pot. We have used a Japanese Black Pine.

6 Using tweezers, carefully remove as much of the soil from the surface and root ball as possible, then tease out the roots. Prune back any very long roots.

7 Put a thin layer of black lava rock in the base of the pot for extra drainage, then pour in a little of the soil mix to the correct height for the root ball of your plant.

8 Position the plant to fit your miniature landscape design— it doesn't have to be centered. Here, we're recreating the look of a tree growing out of a mossy hill.

9 Once you're happy with your plant's position, start to fill in around it with the soil mix.

10 Using a dibber, chopstick, or pencil, work the mix into the pot and then press it down with a spatula.

Project Steps

11 Moisten and clean up pieces of moss and position them around the base of the pine. Look to see if the moss is growing in a particular direction and try to add pieces in contrasting directions. Leave a portion of the soil uncovered.

12 To finish, pour a top dressing of black lava rock over the bare piece of soil to create the effect of water and add interesting texture. Smooth over the black lava rock with a spatula and water everything well. A water mister is useful for the moss.

Care Advice

Where to site Place your bonsai outdoors, ideally, since it needs direct but not strong light; if kept inside, you'll need a well-ventilated room. Position where the plant won't dry out. Frost protection is needed in winter, and it shouldn't be kept somewhere too wet.

Watering and feeding Small containers dry out quickly so require regular watering. In spring and fall, water once a day; in summer, twice a day. During winter, water every 2–3 days, but not at night in case the soil freezes. The fertilizer used at planting should last 1–2 years. You can add additional fertilizer by gently mixing it into the soil, but only use a tiny bit, since the idea is to keep the plant from growing too big.

General care To keep your bonsai plant small, prune long growth back to a branch or secondary bud that is going to continue growing; this is especially important with pines. Trim back long roots every 2–3 years in early spring. Repot when the plant fills the pot and roots come through the drainage hole.

Moss Pots

Celebrate nature in a teacup by creating
miniature moss hills and mountains
adorned with trees. These whimsical
gems are perfect to enjoy in the smallest
of spaces at home or at work.

Project Steps

TOOLS & EQUIPMENT

akadama (baked clay particles), keto
(peat clay) & black lava rock
particles, mixed at a ratio of 3:1:1

large bowl for mixing soils

bonsai or general-purpose fertilizer

teacups with drainage holes drilled
into the bottom using an electric
drill & ceramic drill bit

plastic mesh

scissors

aluminum wire

wire cutters

bonsai or ordinary tweezers

small scoop

dibber, chopstick, or pencil

water mister

PLANT LIST

compact moss, such as woodland
or carpet types

Cotoneaster horizontalis (bottom
right)

Cyclamen hederifolium (bottom left)

Rhus succedeana (Japanese Sumac;
top left)

1 Mix your soils, then add a little
bonsai or general-purpose
fertilizer. Cut a square of mesh to
size for your teacup. Snip a short
section of aluminum wire, bend it
into a U-shape and insert through
the middle of the mesh.

2 Position the mesh over the
drainage hole and bend the
ends of the wire so that they
are flush with the bottom of the
cup. Put a thin layer of black lava
rock particles over the base of the
container for additional drainage.

3 Gently remove soil from the
root ball and tease out the roots
of the cyclamen with tweezers.
Scoop enough soil into the cup so
that the plant sits proud of the rim.

4 Build up the soil into a hill
around the plant. Moisten and
clean up pieces of moss and press
them over the soil, tucking them
into the rim. Mist everything well.

Select teacups that show off the plants and work well as a set

TOOLS & EQUIPMENT

selection of aquarium gravel in contrasting colors and sizes

large, transparent glass or plastic bowl

selection of pebbles

smaller bowl or other container

rainwater or distilled water

shells

PLANT LIST

Eleocharis acicularis

Equisetum japonicum

Myriophyllum aquaticum

Sisyrinchium angustifolium

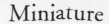

Miniature
Tabletop
Water Garden

This little container garden means you can enjoy a water feature in the smallest of spaces. Ask your aquatics supplier for advice on plants suitable for smaller containers and shallow depths of water.

 TIME IT RIGHT Best to plant in growing season during spring and summer. Plants will last 1–2 years before needing to be transferred to a larger container. Floating plants may outgrow the space more quickly.

1 Carefully take plants out of their pots and remove as much soil as you can while minimizing any damage to the root systems.

2 To loosen the soil and make it easier to remove, you can also soak the plants in room temperature water.

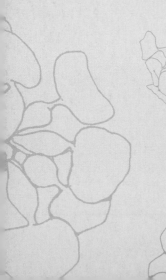

Project Steps

3 Keeping them separate, thoroughly wash the two types of gravel to remove any mud that would dirty the water. Add one type of gravel to the large bowl. Build it up on one side to create a platform for marginal plants that don't set in deep water.

4 Once you have your built-up area of gravel, use clean pebbles to help hold it in place and to separate the two areas in your container.

5 Position a smaller bowl or container, also filled with gravel, on top of the built-up section of gravel to create the planting area for your marginal plants.

6 Add the second, contrasting gravel to your large bowl on the other side of the pebble divide.

7 Plant the lower-level and marginal plants by simply burying their roots in the gravel.

8 Fill the container with rainwater or distilled water. It will look cloudy at first, but will turn clear as the particles settle. Drop the floating plants into the water and decorate with more pebbles and shells until you are happy with the finished result.

Care Advice

Where to site Place where it will receive 4–6 hours of sunlight a day, but do not put in direct sunlight since this may turn the water green. You can keep it outside in summer but do not leave out in freezing conditions.

Feeding and general care Use a slow-release aquatic fertilizer capsule placed directly under the plant in early spring or at planting. Liquid fertilizers tend to discolor the water. Do not feed in fall and winter when plants are dormant. Remove any leaves or other debris, pull off any dead roots from floating water plants, and keep the water levels topped up. Try adding activated carbon granules occasionally, which remove impurities to keep the water clear and sweet smelling.

Occasionally, the water may turn green or brown from foliage decay. When this happens, empty the water out and refill as quickly as possible with rainwater or distilled water.

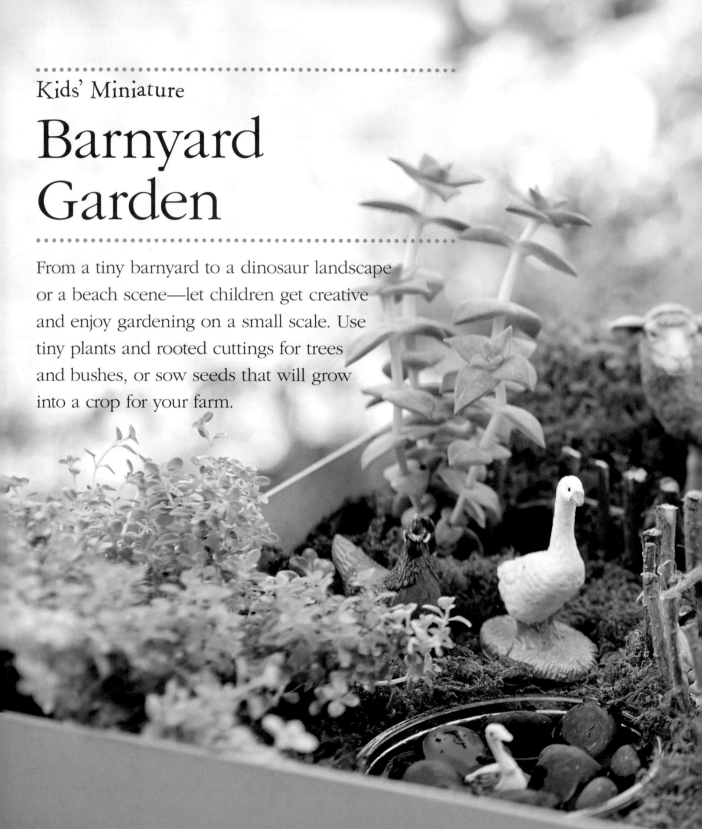

Kids' Miniature

Barnyard Garden

From a tiny barnyard to a dinosaur landscape
or a beach scene—let children get creative
and enjoy gardening on a small scale. Use
tiny plants and rooted cuttings for trees
and bushes, or sow seeds that will grow
into a crop for your farm.

TOOLS & EQUIPMENT

high-sided, loose-bottomed square
  cake pan

gravel

multipurpose potting mix

small glass or plastic container,
  for the pond

blue glass pebbles

small twigs and sticks

scissors

glue gun or multipurpose glue

small aquarium gravel

scraps of material

unripe cherry tomato

selection of small barnyard toys
  and animals

PLANT LIST

carpet moss

cress

Thymus 'Doone Valley'

Thymus praecox 'Elfin'

selection of small foliage plants
  and succulent cuttings

1 A cake pan with a loose bottom
  is perfect for drainage, but add
drainage holes if using a different
container. Cover the base with
a layer of gravel for extra drainage.

2 Add a layer of compost over
  the gravel, gently tapping the
container when all the potting mix
is in to disperse any air and allow
it to settle evenly. Create a mound
for the hill and leave a gap of
2¾in (7cm) from the top of the
container to help with watering.

3 Make a space in the potting
  mix and add the container you
are using for the pond.

4 Add blue glass pebbles to the
  bowl to create your "water."

5 Make a fence by cutting twigs to similar sizes for the uprights, with longer pieces for the cross bars, and glue it all together; a glue gun is useful for this but not essential.

6 Start to lay out your landscaping features, such as the fence, and add pathways made from small aquarium gravel before you start adding plants.

7 Use carpet moss as your "grass" and cover hills and fields, leaving spaces for plants.

8 To make a scarecrow, use a twig for the body, glue two twigs at one end for the legs, then glue another twig horizontally to make the arms. Lay the scarecrow on scraps of material and cut around to make the clothes. Cut out two identical shapes for each item, dab with glue around the edges and stick together. Pop a green tomato on top of the stick for the head.

9 Add plants in scale with your other decorations to act as trees, shrubs, and crops. Finally, add your scarecrow and selection of small toys, and pour some water into the pond.

Care Advice

Watering Plants will need watering once or twice a week, more often in the summer, but do not overwater.

Feeding Add a liquid feed to the water monthly in spring and summer, but do not feed plants during their dormant season and water only sparingly. Place the barnyard on a tray to protect surfaces.

General care Depending on the plants used, you can keep your miniature barnyard outside during spring and summer, but bring inside somewhere cool during fall and winter. Keep plants trimmed, aiming to maintain the shape as natural as possible. Some plants will eventually need to be moved to larger containers when they outgrow their space; simply replace them with smaller plants.

LET IT ALL HANG

TOOLS & EQUIPMENT

planks of wood

handsaw

3 terra-cotta pots with lips, all the same size

tape measure & pencil

electric drill & drill bits

fretsaw or jigsaw

wood clamp

exterior wood paint & paintbrush

clear marine varnish (optional)

blackboard paint & white chalk

crocks or gravel

multipurpose potting mix

watering can

4 lengths of strong but not too thick rope, each at least 6ft (2m) long

carabiner or other strong metal hoop

strong metal hanging bracket, fixed securely to a wall

heavy-duty scissors

PVC tape

PLANT LIST

Eucalyptus gunnii

Festuca glauca 'Intense Blue'

Juncus spiralis (corkscrew rush)

Hanging
Plant Pot Mobile

A stylish alternative to hanging baskets, this mobile is easy to make and can be personalized by painting the holders, pots, and even the rope. We have used architectural plants for a contemporary effect.

TIME IT RIGHT We've grown plants with interesting foliage that can be planted all year round, but it's best to plant them in fall or early spring. Try annuals, herbs, and small evergreen shrubs, too.

1 Cut the planks into three equal squares, 1¼–1½in (3–4cm) larger than the circumference of the pots. Position a pot in the center and draw around the top edge.

2 Draw another circle within this first circle to match the circumference under the lip of the pots, approximately ½in (1.5cm) inside the larger circle.

Project Steps

3 Drill holes slightly wider than your rope into the four corners of each wooden square.

4 Take a square and clamp it to a sturdy work surface to keep it steady. Drill a pilot hole at a point just inside the smaller circle, large enough to accommodate the fretsaw or jigsaw blade. Thread the blade through the hole and cut all the way around the inner circle. Repeat for the other squares.

6 Before planting your pots, first add a layer of crocks or gravel for drainage, and then fill about halfway with potting mix.

5 Paint each pot holder with exterior wood paint and leave to dry. You can also add a coat of clear marine varnish for extra protection. Paint your pots at the same time; we used blackboard paint and chalk (see page 194).

8 Gather together the four ends of your rope, form a long loop, and then tie this off with a strong knot to leave a 4in (10cm) loop at the top. Attach to the carabiner or metal hoop, and hook this onto the bracket where you will be hanging the planter. A sheltered, sunny, or part-shade location is ideal for these plants.

7 Remove plants from their pots and tease out the roots if they are potbound. Place in the pots. Fill around with potting mix and firm in. Water thoroughly.

9 Take a pot holder and insert the rope ends through the corner holes, feeding through until the holder is roughly where you want the top plant. Tie knots in each rope under the holder to keep it in position. Place the plant in the hole. Adjust the rope knots until level. Repeat with the remaining holders. Cut the rope ends and wrap with PVC tape for a neat finish.

Care Advice

Watering and feeding Water often in the growing season, especially if hot and dry. Add diluted liquid fertilizer monthly from mid-spring to early fall. Do not feed and reduce watering in winter.

General care Remove damaged foliage throughout the growing period. The eucalyptus will need repotting into a larger container eventually. Do not cut back the grass or rush in the spring.

TOOLS & EQUIPMENT

2 large bowls

multi-purpose peat-substitute
    potting mix

akadama (baked clay particles)

bucket of water

water mister

natural string or jute twine

scissors

secure hook

PLANT LIST

carpet moss

Davallia humata tyermanii 'Bunny'

Erigeron karvinskianus

Hosta 'Blue Mouse Ears'

Miscanthus sinensis 'Gold Bar'

Nephrolepis exaltata

Ophiopogon nigrescens

Platycerium bifurcatum

Rhodanthemum 'African Eyes'

sphagnum moss (if dried, soak for
    at least 1 hour first and squeeze
    out excess water before using)

Kokedama
Hanging Garden

Meaning "moss" (koke) and "ball" (dama), kokedama is a Japanese art form that offers a whole new way of displaying house plants. It's intriguing, tranquil, and thoroughly enjoyable to put together.

 TIME IT RIGHT Plants should last 1–2 years and can be kept small by pruning. If roots start to show through, it's time to repot. Almost any plants can be grown but remember some will die off or go dormant in winter, while evergreens provide year-round interest.

1 Take plants out of their pots and remove as much soil as you can over a bowl without damaging the root systems. The aim is to keep the root ball as small as possible, though plants with fibrous roots (such as ferns) will need to keep some soil mix.

2 Take a small amount of sphagnum moss and make a "moss wrap" by rolling the plant's roots in it. Set aside in a shady place and make the ball.

Project Steps

3 In a bowl, mix together 70% peat-like potting mix with 30% akadama soil.

4 Now add water a little at a time and shape into a wet clay-like ball that holds together but is porous, and is large enough to take your plant's root ball.

5 Make a space in the center of the ball with your thumbs to take the plant's moss-covered root ball. Insert the root ball and mold back into a ball or teardrop shape.

6 Start to cover the outside of the ball with carpet moss; both this and sphagnum moss are available from florists and floral suppliers. Dampen the moss with a water mister before using.

7 Take your string or twine and wrap it around the moss ball so that everything is held securely in place. Leave two long strands at either side, or one central strand, for hanging. Then simply hang your kokedama on a secure hook and enjoy.

Care Advice

Where to site Most indoor plants prefer to grow in bright but indirect light, although you can place the kokedama plants outdoors in frost-free weather. Since the plants might drip a little after watering, be careful not to hang them above anything that might be damaged by this. Make sure the place you choose to hang them has easy access for removal, watering, and care.

Watering and feeding You will need to water your kokedama plants regularly in the spring and summer growing season, and sparingly during the fall and winter. You can tell by the weight of the ball if it needs watering; if it feels light, then it does. Fill a bucket or bowl with water, immerse the ball to just below the base of the plant, and let it soak for 3–5 minutes. Remove the ball and gently squeeze out the excess water, then leave to hang over a sink or bowl for any additional water to drain out. This method will provide sufficient water for several days, depending on the air temperature. Add liquid fertilizer, such as kelp extract, to the water during spring and summer, but do not feed in fall and winter when plants are dormant.

General care Keep the plants in shape by trimming and pruning, making sure you remove any trimmed foliage. Check that the binding string is secure and not rotting; replace with new string if necessary. Remove any dead, diseased, and dying foliage to keep the plant healthy. Repot any plant that is outgrowing the moss ball into a larger container, or plant outside in a border.

To water your kokedama plant, fill a bucket or bowl with water and fully immerse the moss ball for 3–5 minutes.

Remove the ball and gently squeeze out excess water, then leave it to drain over a sink or bowl before rehanging.

Rhodanthemum
'African Eyes'

Ophiopogon nigrescens

Nephrolepis exaltata

Erigeron karvinskianus

Miscanthus sinensis
'Gold Bar'

*Platycerium
bifurcatum*

Davallia humata tyermanii
'Bunny'

*Hosta
'Blue Mouse Ears'*

TOOLS & EQUIPMENT

oilcloth, single-sided

tape measure

metal rivet kit for fabrics, with post long enough to penetrate several layers of the oilcloth

hammer

plastic-coated images in attractive designs (we cut them from a woven carrier bag) (optional)

scissors

waterproof PVA glue or superglue, jar & paintbrush (optional)

hanging basket liner, cut from a roll

water-retaining gel

multipurpose potting mix

watering can

PLANT LIST

English lavender

French lavender 'Papillon'

Nemesia denticulata 'Confetti'

Pelargonium 'Attar of Roses'

Pelargonium graveolens 'Minor'

rosemary

sage 'Tricolor'

strawberry 'Elan'

Viola 'Blue Beacon'

Saddlebag
Balcony Planters

Only have a balcony as your garden space? These no-sew, easy-to-make saddlebag planters will give you lots of planting space for flowers, herbs, and edibles, and they look stylish and colorful, too.

TIME IT RIGHT We used a selection of herbs, soft fruit, and edible flowers that can be planted in early spring and summer. Add spring bulbs for color and small evergreen shrubs for year-round interest.

2 Fold in one of the short ends by ¾in (2cm) and repeat twice more to create a seam.

1 Use a piece of oilcloth measuring 3ft 3¼in x 4ft (100 x 120cm) and fold in half neatly along the shorter edge with the pattern on the outside.

Project Steps

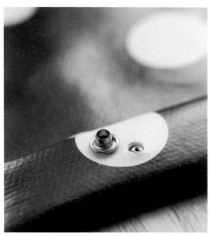

3 Rivet the seam in place, starting 4in (10cm) in from the edge. To make a rivet hole in the cloth, place the plastic disc underneath and hammer the recessed end of the hole punch through the cloth.

4 Push the rivet post through the hole from underneath and tap the cap in place with the hammer. Add three more evenly spaced rivets to the seam, finishing 4in (10cm) in from the other side. Repeat steps 2–4 at the opposite short end.

5 Fold in the riveted ends, leaving enough material in the middle to allow for the width of your railing, so the bags can hang comfortably with the tops of the pockets just below the railing.

6 Flip the cloth over. Fold in a long side twice, including the pocket flaps, to make a 1¼in (3cm) seam. Weight the seam down to hold it as you rivet it in place.

7 Repeat with the other long side. Flip the cloth back over and you have made your saddlebag planters. Repeat to make as many as you need to complete the look.

8 For extra ornamentation, you can cut out some designs from decorative reusable shopping bags to add to the saddlebags.

9 Glue the designs on to the saddlebags with a waterproof PVA glue or superglue and then leave to dry.

10 Take a length of hanging basket liner and line each of the planting pockets, cutting the liner to size with scissors. It should set just below the lip of the pocket. This will help keep the potting mix moist in the pockets. To conserve moisture further, add ¼oz (5g) of water-retaining gel to every 1 gallon (5 liters) of potting mix.

11 Hang the bags in their final locations. Remove plants from their pots, tease out any circling roots, then position them in the pockets. Fill around with potting mix and firm in. Water thoroughly.

Care Advice

Watering Containers above ground level are more exposed and plants tend to dry out more easily, so water often in the growing season, especially if hot and sunny, and while plants are establishing.

Feeding Add diluted liquid fertilizer to the water once or twice a month in the main growing season. You can also mist plants in hot weather, but not when in direct hot sunlight because the leaves might scorch.

General care Remove any damaged, diseased, or dying foliage throughout the growing period. Some plants are not frost hardy and will die back if left outside in winter. Reduce watering in winter to minimal. Top off or change the potting mix in spring.

Balconies can be blooming with these easy, pretty, and practical saddlebag planters

TOOLS & EQUIPMENT

pack of fabric pocket planters (our
 wall required 6 panels)

cable ties

strong bamboo or wooden pole

handsaw or lopper

exterior wood paint & paintbrush

strong garden wire

wire cutters

strong metal hanging brackets,
 fixed securely to a wall

multipurpose potting mix

water-retaining gel

watering can

PLANT LIST

alpine strawberry

Campanula 'Blue Planet'

garlic chives

golden French oregano

lemon thyme

rosemary

sage 'Tricolor'

sweet pepper 'Mohawk Orange'

Viola 'Penny Orange Jump-Up'

Viola 'White Pink Wing'

Edible

Planted Wall

A wall on a porch, veranda, balcony, or walkway
shouldn't be left bare of plants. Think vertically and
hang a carpet of pretty plants up the wall, all
growing in their own special, individual pockets.

TIME IT RIGHT We've grown a mix of herbs,
soft fruit, vegetables, and ornamental plants with
edible flowers that can be planted in early spring to
allow them to mature for summer and fall interest.

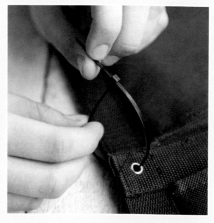

1 Take two panels of fabric
pocket planters and overlap
them along one of their long edges.

2 To join them together, align
the top set of metal eyes
and thread the end of a cable tie
through them. Tie it off at the back
for a neater finish. Tie securely but
not too tightly or you risk bunching
up the fabric.

Project Steps

3 Repeat with the middle eyes, but leave the bottom eyes free for now; you will need to overlap the second row of panels before tying off. Build up the panels until you have the planter the right size.

4 Cut a sturdy bamboo cane or wooden pole to size with a handsaw or lopper and paint it in a matching color using exterior wood paint. Leave to dry, then attach the pole to the top of the planting wall with cable ties threaded through the free eyes along the top row of the panels.

5 Loop strong garden wire several times around the pole at either side of the hanging wall, leaving long lengths of wire at each end. Tie these ends securely to sturdy brackets and hang the planting wall.

6 The soil mix in the pockets can quickly dry out, so to help conserve moisture add ¼oz (5g) of water-retaining gel to every 1 gallon (5 liters) of potting mix.

7 Remove each plant from its pot, gently teasing out the roots if they are circling. Insert into a pocket; you may need to reduce the root ball by removing some of the earth for it to fit. Fill around with soil mix and firm in. Water well.

Care Advice

Watering Water often during the growing season, especially if hot and sunny and while plants are establishing. Use a watering can with a long spout to get water directly into each pouch, but do not overwater so that soil spills out. Mist for extra moisture, but not when in direct hot sunlight or the leaves might scorch.

Feeding Add diluted liquid feed to the water monthly in the growing season and also mist with the mixture, avoiding any scorching sun.

General care Remove damaged foliage in the growing period. Some plants will need to be planted into larger containers eventually. Reduce watering in winter to minimal. Top off or change the potting mix in the spring.

Deadhead flowering plants regularly to encourage production of more flowers.

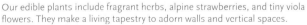

Our edible plants include fragrant herbs, alpine strawberries, and tiny viola flowers. They make a living tapestry to adorn walls and vertical spaces.

TOOLS & EQUIPMENT

2 coir-lined hanging baskets

plastic pot or bucket

small bag of vermiculite or perlite

wooden board or piece of stiff
  cardboard

garden wire

wire cutters

long-handled screwdriver

chopstick, dibber, or pencil

hairpins or florist mossing pins

heavy-duty chain & swivel hook

PLANT LIST

approx. 100 cuttings or offsets from
  10–15 succulent plants, choosing a
  mix of shape and color from the
  following genera:
  Echeveria
  Graptopetalum
  x *Graptoveria*
  Sedum
  Sempervivum

sphagnum moss

Hanging Ball of Succulents

Why just hang a basket when you can hang a living ball of contemporary art? Stylish and undemanding, succulents are perfect if you want a high-impact display, but don't have much time for plant care.

TIME IT RIGHT Plants will start to root quickly, but it will take 4–6 months for the ball to fill out completely. A smaller ball will take less time. Do not plant in winter when succulents become dormant.

Project Steps

1 Gather your materials and find a firm, level surface to work on. Remove the metal chains from the hanging baskets and set them aside since they are not required for this project. Position one of the wire baskets in a plastic pot just big enough to hold it.

2 If using dried sphagnum moss, soak it in water for at least an hour before using. Remove from the water and squeeze out any excess, then pack a layer of moss at least 2in (5cm) thick into the base and sides of the basket.

3 Fill with vermiculite (or perlite), packing it in tightly to just below the top of the moss. The vermiculite provides a lightweight filling for the ball; the plants will root into the moss as they grow.

Project Steps

Succulents are plants that store water in their fleshy leaves and naturally thrive in dry climates

4 Cover the top of the vermiculite with another thick layer of moss. Pack it in well and then set aside the first basket. Repeat the process with the second basket. Place a wooden board (or piece of stiff cardboard) over the first basket and carefully flip it upside down, then place it over the second basket and align the sides. Working quickly but carefully, pull the board out from between the two baskets.

5 Firmly tie together the baskets by cutting a length of flexible garden wire using wire cutters and threading it around the two edges. Secure with several tight knots.

x Graptoveria 'Fred Ives'

Echeveria 'Topsy Turvy'

Graptopetalum 'Paraguayense'

Echeveria shaviana

Sempervivum 'Pippin'

Sedeveria 'Letizia'

x Graptoveria 'Fred Ives'

Sedum commixtum

Echeveria elegans

6 Cuttings of little plants called offsets, which grow from the main plant, are used. You need to make the stem as long as you can on the offset, then pare the end to a point. Ideally, take cuttings two days in advance to allow the cut ends to dry a little before planting—this helps with rooting. Twist together a length of garden wire around any short stems.

Sedum morganianum

Sempervivum 'Kelly Jo'

Project Steps

PLANTING TIPS

Adding twisted wire tails to cuttings with short or floppy stems will help to anchor them. A chopstick or dibber is perfect for teasing the stems into the planting holes. Fix any loose cuttings in place with hairpins or moss pins.

7 Plant the top half of the ball first. Make planting holes by inserting the end of a long-handled screwdriver. Position the holes roughly 2in (5cm) apart. Leave the ball for 10 days in a bright location to allow the cuttings to set roots; if you try planting both sides at once, the cuttings will fall out when you turn it over.

8 When ready to plant the second half, first immerse the whole ball in water for a minute and let it drip. Then, with the bare side facing up for planting, attach a heavy-duty metal chain at the top center of the basket. Fix a swivel hook to the other end of the chain so the ball can rotate. Hang in a secure place and finish planting.

Care Advice

Where to site
Succulents don't like a lot of humidity. They are happy outside in the summer if sheltered from rain, but they can't withstand freezing and prolonged wet conditions. Ideally, keep your succulent ball in a frost-free location inside from mid-fall to early spring, although they can tolerate cooler temperatures in a sheltered porch as long as it doesn't freeze. Do not water the ball during this dormant period since it could encourage the plants to rot.

Watering
Give the ball a thorough soaking in the growing season by immersing in a bucket of water for no longer than 20 minutes, then allow to drain before rehanging. Start with one immersion in late March/early April, then repeat monthly until the end of May and every two weeks in summer. Take care not to overwater. Immerse monthly beginning in September, but not from November to March since the plants are then dormant.

Feeding
Apply a diluted feed to the plants by adding liquid fertilizer (such as kelp extract) to the water when you immerse the ball. Measure how much water your bucket will hold and check the manufacturer's instructions on the liquid fertilizer label to ensure the correct dilution. Only feed during spring and summer and at the same time as watering. Do not feed in fall and winter.

General care
Trim or prune plants to keep the ball neat and maintain its shape. Plants may need pruning as they start to produce offsets and outgrow their location. Snip off any excess plant material and use as cuttings, potting them into free-draining gritty mix after allowing two days for them to dry out. Trim any spent flowering stalks back to the plant base and remove any dead material before winter since this could attract disease if left.

Immerse your succulent ball completely in a bucket of water with added liquid feed. Leave to drain afterward.

Snip off spent flower heads and remove overgrown plants. Tweezers are excellent for picking off dead leaves.

TOOLS & EQUIPMENT

old metal tray

pond liner or similar & scissors

strong outdoor adhesive & paintbrush

vintage teacups, teapot, and creamer

masking tape

electric drill & ceramic drill bit

gravel & small scoop or spoon

soil-based potting mix

horticultural grit

slow-release fertilizer granules

strong galvanized chain

wire cutters

3 small galvanized metal hooks

large galvanized metal ring

strong metal hanging bracket,
   fixed securely to a wall

vintage cutlery (optional)

silver florist wire or similar (optional)

PLANT LIST

Armeria juniperifolia
   'Bevan's Variety'

carpet moss

Erigeron karvinskianus

Pratia peduncularis

Rhodohypoxis deflexa

Sisyrinchium californicum
   'Brachypus'

Vintage

Teatime Alpine Planter

Enjoy English afternoon tea in the garden with this delicate tray and vintage tea set filled with delicate alpine plants. This fun project is quick and easy to make and brings a welcoming touch to your home.

 TIME IT RIGHT Enjoy your tea set all year round with seasonal planting: alpine bulbs in spring and fall; mossy alpines or dwarf ivy in winter, and with fairy lights for a festive look.

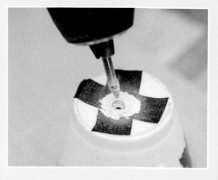

1 Cut a piece of pond liner (or you could use a heavy-duty garbage bag) to fit inside the base of the tray. Glue it into place with outdoor adhesive.

2 Take your cups, teapot, and creamer and make a cross with two pieces of masking tape over the center area where you intend to drill a hole; this helps prevent the drill from slipping and creates a clean cut. Drill drainage holes in the base of the items using an electric drill with a ceramic tile drill bit.

3 Select alpine plants to fit in the tea set. Look for different heights, leaf shapes, and flowers.

Project Steps

4 Create an attractive arrangement with your tea set on the lined tray and then glue the saucers in place and remove the cups, teapot, and creamer for planting.

5 Alpines need good drainage, so to plant, first fill the base of each piece with a layer of gravel. Next, make a soil medium suitable for alpine plants by blending soil-based potting mix with horticultural grit at a ratio of 3:1. At the same time, mix in a small amount of slow-release fertilizer.

6 Add potting mix to your pieces until the plant sits at the right height, and fill around it with more mix, finishing with a layer of gravel. Water in using a fine nozzle.

Project Steps

7 Place the planted cups on saucers and the other items on the tray and glue in place; just dab glue on one or two spots on the bottom of the cups to leave space for water to drain into the saucers. Fill around each piece with moss.

 ## Care Advice

 Where to site Alpines prefer a sunny site that is not too shady and, ideally for this arrangement, one that has shelter from strong winds. In winter and freezing weather, bring your teatime planter indoors, but keep it in a cool, light place.

Watering and feeding
Alpines thrive in dry conditions in the natural world so don't overwater—just when needed from mid-spring to early fall, with occasional watering at other times. Do not let plants sit in water for long periods of time or this could lead to rot. Alpines do not need a lot of fertilizer so it is best to give a weak diluted liquid fertilizer during the growing season. Do not feed when the plants are dormant.

 General care Trim or prune plants with small scissors or pruners to remove spent flower stalks and dead material. Plants will eventually outgrow their teacups so plant them into larger containers or borders elsewhere in the garden.

8 To hang, cut three lengths of chain to the desired hanging height using wire cutters. Attach to hooks and then to the edge of the tray. Gather the chains and fix the free ends to a ring. Hang from a strong bracket. If you like, decorate the chains by attaching vintage pieces of cutlery with fine silver wire.

Succulents, such as the sempervivums shown top left and bottom right, also look pretty in teacups and require similar growing conditions and care.

TOOLS & EQUIPMENT

pendant lampshade in opaque plastic, large enough to fit a small plant bag—ours was 15in (38cm) in diameter and 71in (180cm) in height

tape measure

small hacksaw

wooden dowel, ½in (1.5cm) diameter

electric drill & drill bits

wood screws

large metal cup hook

small plant bag with handles

scissors

hanging basket liner

multipurpose potting mix

slow-release fertilizer granules

S-hook

garden wire

wire cutters

PLANT LIST

chile pepper 'Loco'

chile pepper 'Razzamatazz'

Upside-down
Lampshade Chile Planter

Turn your plants on their heads by growing them upside down in a lampshade. It may look quirky, but some vegetables thrive on this method, and it's ideal if you have limited space to grow things.

 TIME IT RIGHT Young, small plants or seedlings are easier to plant in early to mid-spring. Depending on what you're using, hang in a sheltered, frost-free place until the danger of frost has passed.

1 Measure the internal width of the top opening of the lampshade and, using a small hacksaw, cut a section of wooden dowel to fit this space.

2 Match a drill bit to the size of your screws and drill two holes opposite each other through the lip of the top opening of the lampshade, near the outer edge.

Project Steps

3 Holding the section of dowel under the drilled holes and flush against the top opening, drill screws through the holes and firmly into the dowel.

4 Turn the lampshade over. Match a drill bit to the width of the cup hook and drill a shallow hole into the center of the dowel, to help screw in the hook.

5 Take the plant bag and cut a small cross in the center of the base, just large enough to fit the root ball of your plant.

6 Insert your plant through the cross. Carefully turn the bag over, resting it at the edge of the work surface so the plant hangs over the side.

7 If necessary, stitch together the seams of the opening in the plant bag with garden wire to make the plant more secure. Cut a cross in the hanging basket liner to match the one in the plant bag. Ease the liner over the root ball of the plant, making sure it fits snugly around where the stem comes out of the opening. Trim the liner so it fits inside the bag.

8 Fill around the root ball with potting mix, mixing in a handful of slow-release fertilizer granules. Stop when three-quarters full to allow space for watering.

9 Lift the plant bag into the lampshade and hang it by the handles from the cup hook. Put an S-hook under the dowel, or fix it firmly with garden wire, and use the top of the S-hook to hang from a sturdy support.

Care Advice

Where to site Chile peppers need a good amount of sun to ripen, so place the planter in a sunny but sheltered place, where you can easily access the top for watering.

Watering and feeding Water frequently during the growing season and while the plant is establishing, especially if the weather is hot and sunny. Add some diluted liquid fertilizer to the water once or twice a month in the main growing season. Watering is done through the open top of the lampshade directly into the plant bag, so use a watering can with a long spout. You can also mist the plants in hotter weather.

General care Remove damaged or dying foliage during the growing period. Chile peppers are not frost hardy and will die back if left outside in winter. You could try to overwinter your plant by moving it into a light, frost-free place, or simply hang it inside by a sunny window. Reduce watering. Change soil mix in spring—your plant may or may not start to grow new shoots!

TOOLS & EQUIPMENT

clear, strong plastic cups, ours were colored turquoise

soldering iron (optional)

clear-drying superglue

bird feeder globe with hanger, the two halves superglued together and left to dry

air plant fixative (silicone rubber sealant)

masking tape

garden twine, ideally in a color to match the cups

scissors

PLANT LIST

selection of small air plants— the spiky ones look good:
Tillandsia aeranthos
Tillandsia brachycaulos multiflora
Tillandsia ixioides
Tillandsia tectorum

Plastic Cup

Air Plant Chandelier

Versatile, fun, and quirky, air plants don't need any soil to grow in and as such are perfect for growing in unusual decorative features, like this stylish and contemporary living chandelier.

 TIME IT RIGHT Plant your chandelier at any time of the year if you are keeping it inside. Air plants aren't frost hardy, but you can hang it outside for summer, bringing it back indoors in mid-fall.

1 We made holes in the base of the cups using a hot soldering iron, so that when "planted" the air plants seem to sprout from the ends. If you prefer not to do this, simply attach the plants straight to the cup base with silicone glue (see step 3).

2 Work out the best positions of the cups on the globe, so they cover the surface evenly and fit closely together. Apply superglue around the rim of each cup and press in place, holding them until bonded. Leave to dry completely.

Project Steps

3 Attach an air plant to the base of each cup using a silicone rubber sealant (other glues can harm plants). Apply sealant around the rim of the hole, if made, or apply a generous dab in the center. Press the plants in place and avoid getting sealant on the stem end.

4 You can also stick additional plants onto the globe in the spaces between the cups for a fuller effect. The sealant takes several hours to dry and you will need to hold each plant in place as it dries by sticking one or two leaves down with masking tape.

5 Once the sealant has dried completely and the air plants are secure, carefully remove the strips of masking tape. To hang the chandelier, cut a length of garden twine, thread it through the hook of the globe and tie it off with a secure knot.

Care Advice

Where to site Air plants like warmth but not direct sunlight, and you can hang your chandelier outdoors in spring, summer, and early fall. Bring inside during the rest of fall and winter since plants are not hardy below 46°F (8°C). Plants are fine in many areas of the house as long as light levels and air circulation are good and they are kept moist (see below). Do not place them near heat sources.

Watering and feeding Air plants absorb moisture through their leaves and generally need spraying 2–3 times a week, more frequently during summer or in dry conditions, and ideally with rainwater. Give plants a generous soak at least once a month by submerging the entire chandelier in room temperature water for a little while, making sure you shake off excess water afterward. Feed with a diluted air plant liquid fertilizer misted on leaves once a week in spring and summer, twice a month in winter.

General care Remove any dead, diseased, or dying foliage throughout the year and be careful not to let any water sit in the base of the plant since this could cause it to rot. Plants will produce offsets that can be removed when half the size of their mother plant, and then used in other displays.

More ideas for
Air Plant Hangers

You can buy ceramic or clear glass aeriums and terrariums specifically designed for displaying air plants. Simply fill the base with a little sand or gravel for the air plant to set in, or wire on or glue the plants in place with silicone rubber sealant.

Wicker balls also make effective hanging globes. Attach a long piece of florist wire to a plant, position it on one side of the ball, thread the wire through to the other side, pull gently, and tie off.

Hang aeriums and terrariums together in a group to create a tiny air plant world. Try adding florist's moss, shells, or bark to produce a miniature hanging landscape.

You could also attach plants to the ball with silicone sealant. Don't forget to keep your air plants regularly sprayed with water, and immerse the entire ball in water at least once a month.

GROW UP

TOOLS & EQUIPMENT

tape measure, pencil, & ruler

handsaw

marine-grade plywood

old picture frame

electric drill & drill bits

screws

6 heavy-duty metal hanging brackets

PVA glue & water solution (mixed at a ratio of 1:10), jar, & paintbrush

clear marine varnish (optional)

green garden wire

water-retaining gel

multipurpose potting mix

2 pairs of thick, opaque tights

scissors

absorbent dishcloth

cable ties

hanging basket liner, cut from a roll

PLANT LIST

strawberry 'Elan'

strawberry 'Rhapsody'

Strawberry
Picture Frame Planter

Bring life back to an old picture frame by creating planting pockets and filling them with strawberry plants. The picture changes as the plants grow, while flowers and fruit add extra interest and color.

TIME IT RIGHT Create the planting pockets at any time of year, but early to mid-spring is best for planting up strawberries; or for an even earlier crop, plant in fall and keep in a frost-free place over winter.

1 Measure and cut a piece of marine plywood to fit the back of the picture frame. Screw in place, then screw brackets to the plywood at each corner and at the center of the top and bottom edge.

2 Brush the PVA solution over the frame and plywood to help protect them from the elements. Leave to dry. You could also add a final coat of clear marine varnish for extra protection.

Project Steps

3 Mark on the plywood a straight vertical line of four crosses, evenly spaced along one of the long edges of the frame. The lowest cross should start just in from the bottom corner. Repeat at the opposite long edge and then twice more at equal intervals in between. You should have a grid of 16 crosses. Drill a hole, wide enough to hold two lengths of garden wire, at each cross.

PLANTING TIPS

Dainty alpine strawberries are a good choice if your frame is smaller. Alternative plants include tumbler-style tomatoes, seasonal trailing annuals, and herbs. Ivy provides year-round greenery— variegated ivy adds interest.

4 Add water-retaining gel to the soil mix at a ratio of $^1/_4$oz (5g) of gel to every 1 gallon (5 liters) of soil mix. Mix in thoroughly. This will help to hold moisture in the planting tube, but do not use more than necessary since it will push plants out of the potting mix.

5 Cut a pair of tights into separate legs and feed the potting mix into one of them until you have made a planting tube. The tube should be the same length as the inside long edge of the picture frame and should fit comfortably between the lines of holes drilled in the plywood.

6 Cut a piece of absorbent cloth 1¼–1½in (3–4cm) wide and the same length as the planting tube. Feed the cloth down what will be the back of the planting tube—this will act as a wick to help distribute the moisture.

7 Tie off the open end of the tube with a cable tie, then squeeze the soil mix to divide it into four equal sections. Tie off between sections with cable ties. This prevents soil from sinking down the tube.

8 Cut planting holes in the center of each section with scissors and gently open them out a little with your fingers.

⟿ Project Steps

10 Wrap the tube with the liner. Feel where the planting holes are and cut matching holes through the liner with scissors.

9 Cut a piece of hanging basket liner large enough to wrap around the planting tube, allowing a little overlap on the side and a larger overlap at the bottom end.

11 To attach the planting tube to the picture frame, thread lengths of garden wire over the tube and through the holes in the plywood on either side of it. Pull tight and tie off firmly at the back of the frame. The planting tubes are also held in place at the bottom, so make sure the bottom end of the hanging-basket liner is tucked underneath the tube and held firmly in place when tied to the frame. The top end of the tube is left open for watering.

12 Remove the strawberry plants from their pots and carefully pull off most of the soil attached to the root ball. Gently ease each plant into a planting hole and firm in around it.

13 Stitch planting holes with wire if too wide. Repeat steps 5–13 twice more to make three tubes. Water well while flat. Wait for excess water to drain. Attach the frame to your surface by screwing through the brackets.

 ## Care Advice

 Where to site Strawberries need a fair amount of sun for crops to ripen, so choose a sunny but sheltered spot.

 Watering and feeding Water frequently in growing season and while plants are getting established. Add diluted liquid fertilizer to the water once or twice a month. In winter, reduce watering and do not feed. Use a watering can with a long spout to water. You can also mist plants in hotter weather.

 General care Remove damaged or dying foliage or fruit in the growing period. Cut back after fruiting and pot any runners (see page 159). You may need to net the frame to protect fruit from birds.

Use a watering can with a long spout to get water directly into the soil at the top of each planting tube.

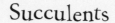

TOOLS & EQUIPMENT

compass & pencil

electric jigsaw

large piece of particle board

round mirror

exterior wood paint & paintbrushes

clear marine varnish (optional)

greenhouse shading material

craft knife

staple gun

chopstick, dibber, or pencil

hairpins or florist mossing pins

garden wire & wire cutters

strong outdoor adhesive

nails & sturdy brass picture hook

hammer

PLANT LIST

approximately 50 cuttings or offsets
  from a range of succulent plants,
  choosing a mix of shape and color
  from the following genera:
  Echeveria
  Graptopetalum
  Pachyphytum
  Sedum
  Sempervivum

sphagnum moss

Succulents

Living Mirror Frame

Succulent plants are easy to look after and demand little attention. This stunning living wreath provides a glamorous frame for a mirror and creates impact wherever it is placed.

 TIME IT RIGHT Plants will root quickly but it will take 3–5 months for the frame to fill out completely. It's best started in mid-spring when plants come out of their winter dormancy and will be actively growing.

1 Using a compass and pencil and a jigsaw, cut a piece of particle board to the shape of your mirror, allowing a 6¾in (17cm) border all around. Paint the board, leave to dry, then apply a coat of marine varnish for added protection, if preferred. Once dry, draw around the mirror onto the board to create a guideline, but do not attach it at this stage.

Sedum brevifolia

Sedum dasyphyllum

Sempervivum 'Grapetone'

Sempervirum 'Dark Cloud'

Sempervivum 'Rosie'

Echeveria elegans

Sedum sexangulare

Sedum album 'Coral Carpet'

Project Steps

2 To make the planting tube, carefully cut the shading material using a craft knife to twice the width of your border. Aligning one edge with the guideline, attach the mesh using a staple gun, pleating it to fit the circle.

3 Fold over the mesh and start to form the planting tube shape. Fill with dampened sphagnum moss and, as you do so, fold over the mesh, tucking under the loose edge, and staple it down to form the tube.

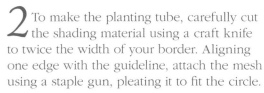

4 Prepare plants ideally a few days before planting to dry the stems and aid rooting. Take the plants out of their pots and remove most of the planting mix; with crowded pots it may be easiest to slice off any root ball beyond the planting depth required.

5 Separate plants into offsets or cuttings so you are left with a single longish stem. Using a utility knife, cut the stems to size, then pare the ends to a point. Fix short or floppy stems with hairpins or by attaching twists of wire as tails.

Care Advice

Watering and feeding
Use a water mister to water gently between the plants into the sphagnum moss, trying to avoid getting water on the leaves if possible. Water about every 10 days in summer; add a diluted liquid fertilizer to the water during spring and summer. Do not feed or water in fall and winter.

General care
We used *Echeveria*, which isn't frost hardy, so the frame should overwinter in a sheltered porch or similar; if very wet and cold, move somewhere more protected, cool, and bright. Plants may need pruning as they start to produce offsets and outgrow their position. Simply snip off excess plant material and use as cuttings. Remove spent flower stalks and dead material before winter as this could attract disease.

Excess plant trimmings are ideal for cuttings. Pot them into free-draining gritty potting mix after you've given them a couple days to dry out.

6 Use a dibber to pierce planting holes, 2in (5cm) apart, through the mesh and into the moss. Plant the frame, making sure the cuttings set flush with the mesh.

7 Once planted, leave the frame somewhere flat for two weeks to allow the plants to root in. Attach the mirror using a strong outdoor adhesive and nail a brass picture hook onto the back of the frame to hang your succulent mirror.

Succulents

Living Picture Frame

Easy to look after and, once rooted, happy growing vertically, succulents are a good choice for living pictures. Start your decorative display by using small succulent cuttings or offsets, then watch your picture grow and evolve over the seasons.

 TIME IT RIGHT Plants will start to root quickly, but it will take 4–6 months for the frame to fill out and be completely covered. Do not plant in winter when succulents become dormant.

TOOLS & EQUIPMENT

wooden box-style picture frame in
  2 parts, ideally 2in (5cm) deep and
  with an overlapping front

4–6 strong metal hanging brackets

electric drill & screws

emulsion paint mixed 2:1 with PVA

paintbrushes

clear marine varnish (optional)

heavy-duty plastic liner & scissors

exterior glue or staplegun

tape measure

wooden batten & handsaw

soil-based potting mix & perlite

bucket & trowel

micromesh

wood filler & sandpaper (optional)

dibber, chopstick, or pencil

PLANT LIST

selection of succulent cuttings:
  Echeveria elegans
  Echeveria secunda glauca
  Sedum spathulifolium 'Purpureum'
  Sempervivum arachnoideum
  Sempervivum 'Blue Boy'
  Sempervivum calcareum
  Sempervivum 'Pilatus'
sphagnum moss (soaked 1 hour, if dry)

Project Steps

1 Buy or make your own box frame, 2in (5cm) deep
  to allow space for the soil, but no deeper or the
frame starts to become too heavy; ours measured
31½ x 23½ x 2in (80 x 60 x 5cm). Screw brackets in
the four corners of the box frame and two more in the
center of each long edge for extra stability, if preferred.

2 Paint the box and front frame
  with a PVA and emulsion mix
to help protect against the elements.
Leave to dry, add another coat if
required, then apply a finishing
coat of clear marine varnish for
additional protection, if preferred.

3 Cut plastic liner so that it lines
  the insides of the box, right up
to the edge of the frame. Measure
and cut 2 pieces of batten so they
sit parallel to the top of the frame.

4 Position the batten so they are evenly spaced, and screw them to the box frame. This creates planting compartments to prevent the soil from slipping down to the bottom once the frame is hung.

5 In a large bucket, mix up a free-draining growing medium for the succulent plants of 2 parts soil-based potting mix to 1 part perlite. Do not use ordinary potting mix since it retains too much moisture, which would eventually rot the roots of the plants.

6 Fill each of the planting compartments with the soil mix to just below the top edge of the box frame. Lightly tap down the whole frame so that the soil settles and the surface is level.

Project Steps

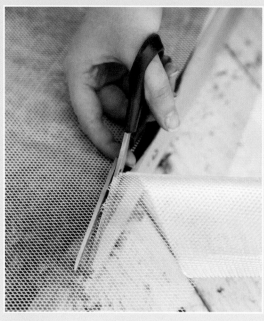

7 Squeeze out excess water from the sphagnum moss and put a thick layer over the top of the soil mix. The moss will help the succulent plants to root in.

8 Cut a piece of micromesh to overlap the edge of the box frame; this allows the mesh to be held in place when the front is screwed on.

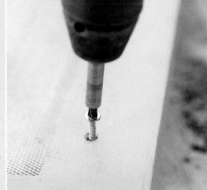

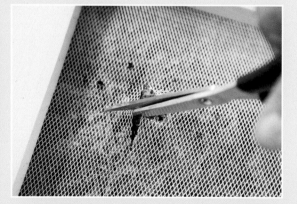

9 Screw the front onto the box frame, ensuring the micromesh is held securely in place. Paint over the screws or, for a neater finish, drill a recess hole for each screw, cover the screw head with wood filler, sand smooth, then paint over.

10 Plan your planting design; we aimed to create bands of color with blocks of each particular succulent. To make a planting hole, cut a cross in the mesh with a pair of scissors.

11 Fold back the sides of the cross, then insert your plant dibber to create a planting hole. Place your plant into the hole, firm soil around the roots and then fold back the edge of the mesh.

12 Plant succulents 1¼–2in (3–5cm) apart; over 4–6 months they will produce further plantlets to fill in the picture. Leave the frame flat for one to two weeks until the plants have put down roots, before securely screwing the frame to its final hanging location.

Care Advice

Where to site We used *Echeveria*, which isn't frost hardy, so our frame needs to come inside somewhere cool and bright in mid-fall and over winter. If all plants are hardy, leave the frame outside all year, but if the winter is very wet, move it somewhere more protected from heavy downpours, like a sheltered porch.

Watering and feeding Use a water mister to squirt water into the moss between the plants, trying to avoid getting water on the succulent leaves. Water every 10 days in summer and add a diluted liquid fertilizer to the water in spring and summer, but do not feed in fall and winter, and do not water in winter.

General care Snip spent flowering stalks back to the base and remove any dead plant material before winter, since this could attract disease. Plants may need pruning as they grow larger. Simply snip off any excess plant material and use as cuttings.

Air Plants

Living Picture Frame

Make an eye-catching vertical display of plants that seem to float in the air. Tillandsia air plants get all their moisture and nutrients from the air, making them perfect for creating some living art.

TIME IT RIGHT Air plants aren't frost hardy so make your living picture frame inside during late spring, which will give plants time to anchor onto the support wires. Put the frame outside for summer, bringing it back indoors in mid-fall.

A Rootless Life

Tillandsias are known as air plants because they are able to grow without soil, getting moisture and nutrients from the air through specially adapted leaves. Plants that are watered and fed well will reward you with flowers and new plants, which appear in the form of offsets or "pups." Leave the pups to form clumps or remove them when half the size of the parent plant for use in other displays.

Air plants grow short roots only in order to attach themselves to their host object.

TOOLS & EQUIPMENT

wooden box-style picture frame,
  ideally 2in (5cm) deep and with an
  overlapping front, painted with a
  2:1 mix of emulsion paint and PVA
  glue, finished with a coat of clear
  marine varnish (see page 120)

pencil & tape measure

electric drill & drill bits

screw eyes

strong metal hanging brackets

screws

galvanized wire

pliers

wire cutters

florist wire

PLANT LIST

selection of small air plants, such as:
  Tillandsia aeranthos
  Tillandsia bulbosa
  Tillandsia circinnata
  Tillandsia filifolia
  Tillandsia ionantha
  Tillandsia ionantha scaposa
  Tillandsia ixioides
  Tillandsia juncea
  Tillandsia melanocrater tricolor
  Tillandsia tectorum

Project Steps

1 Measure and mark points for holes for the screw eyes all the way around the inside edge of the box frame, about ¾in (2cm) behind the front frame and at 4–6in (10–15cm) intervals. Match a drill bit to the width of the screw eyes and drill shallow holes at each of the marked points.

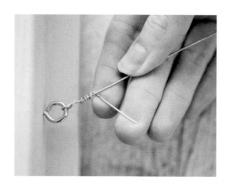

3 Take one end of a coil of galvanized wire, thread a short length of 1¼–2in (3–5cm) through one of the screw eyes, and twist it back around the wire to secure it.

2 Twist in screw eyes by hand at each of the drilled starter holes. Screw heavy-duty metal hanging brackets in the four corners of the box frame, plus a third bracket in the center of each long edge, if preferred, for additional security.

4 Uncoil enough wire to reach an eye hook diagonally opposite on the frame, leaving 1¼–2in (3–5cm) excess. Cut with wire cutters. Thread the loose end through the eye and, using pliers, pull it so that the length of wire is taut across the frame. Twist off and secure; there should be no slack.

5 Repeat to create an abstract "mesh" with areas of fairly closely overlapping wires where the air plants can easily be attached. Affix several wires to each screw eye, if required.

6 Wrap florist wire around the plant stems to secure them to the mesh structure. If a plant has a short stem, gently slide the wire between the bottom pair of leaves.

7 Attach plants by tucking the leaves between wires and tying off with the florist wire. The plant will eventually secure itself to the wire by anchoring with a root. Securely fix your frame onto a sturdy surface using the brackets.

Care Advice

Where to site Air plants like warmth but not direct sunlight and are happy outdoors in spring, summer, and early fall. Bring your frame inside when temperatures fall below 46°F (8°C), somewhere with good light levels and air circulation; do not place near registers.

Watering and feeding Air plants absorb moisture and nutrients from the air through their leaves. Plants generally need spraying 2–3 times a week (ideally using rainwater), more frequently during summer or dry conditions. Feed with a diluted air plant liquid fertilizer misted on leaves once a week in spring and summer, twice a month in winter.

General care Remove dead, diseased, or dying foliage throughout the year. Do not let water sit in the base of the plant.

TOOLS & EQUIPMENT

non-PVC plastic gutter kit,
 with brackets and end pieces

tape measure & pencil

hacksaw or handsaw

electric drill & drill bits

face mask (optional)

nontoxic spray paint (optional),
 marked as suitable for exterior
 use and safe for children's toys
 and furniture

screws

multipurpose potting mix & scoop

well-rotted manure

watering can

PLANT LIST

whole dried Alaska peas & dried
 broad beans from a supermarket,
 pre-soaked for 24 hours

Pea and Broad Bean

Shooter Shelves

Transform ordinary plastic gutters into an attractive and innovative growing space for a tasty, nutritious crop of salad shoots—a fun way to use vertical space for growing vegetables.

 TIME IT RIGHT Sow dried peas and beans from spring through to fall. Protect emerging shoots from frost and freezing weather. If conditions are right, you can expect to be harvesting shoots in 4–6 weeks.

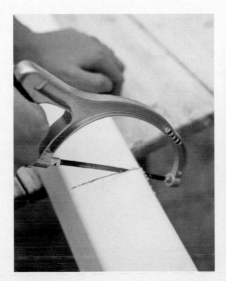

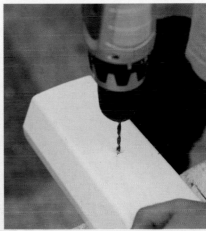

1 Measure the gutters to your desired lengths, mark with a pencil, then carefully cut to size using a hacksaw or handsaw.

2 To provide some drainage, drill small holes in the base of each length of gutter, roughly 29½in (75cm) apart, using an electric drill and relatively thin drill bit.

Project Steps

3 If you like, paint the gutters in a color of your choice. The easiest way to do this is using a nontoxic spray paint. Apply in a ventilated room or outside and wear a face mask to avoid breathing in any paint. Leave to dry completely.

4 Mark the location of the brackets on the wall so that they are carefully aligned. Keep in mind ease of access for watering and harvesting, and make sure the shoots have space to grow up to at least 8in (20cm). Screw the brackets to the wall, attach the end pieces, and then click into place.

5 Make a soil mix of equal proportions of multipurpose potting mix and manure, then fill the gutter to a little below the top lip, leaving space for watering. Water the soil well.

6 Sow the presoaked peas and beans in separate planting blocks. Since you are only growing them for shoots, you can sow them much closer together than for mature plants.

7 Cover thinly with more of the soil mix. Green shoots should start to appear after a week, depending on conditions and temperature.

8 The optimal time to harvest shoots is when they are 4–8in (10–20cm) high; any longer and the shoots start to get tough. Carefully pinch shoots off halfway to two-thirds down the plant, just above a leaf joint; this will encourage the plant to grow more shoots for a second harvest.

 ## Care Advice

 Where to site Preferably in a sheltered location, the shoots will need some sunlight but will be happy in a semishade location.

 **Watering** Water frequently or daily, depending on conditions, once shoots start to appear. Never let the soil mix dry out, which can easily happen with a shallow container. Feeding is not required.

TOOLS & EQUIPMENT

2 wooden wine gift boxes (4-bottle)

strong outdoor adhesive

metal clamps

electric drill, drill bits & screws

small handsaw

wooden batten

pencil, pen & ruler

wooden rounded architrave

additional piece of wood, for lid

4 metal hinges

exterior wood paint & paintbrushes

clear marine varnish (optional)

sheet of acrylic glass & silicone glue

cupboard door knob

square wooden batten

4 mirror fixing plates

2 door hooks

newspaper & aerosol can with good
   recess at the base, for seed pots

PLANT LIST

easy seedlings to try are: lettuce,
   beans, and annual flowers—start
   seeds in recycled clear plastic food
   trays (add drainage holes), then
   grow seedlings in newspaper pots

*Alchemilla mollis, Digitalis purpurea,
Dryopteris filix-mas,* and *Primula
vialii* are planted underneath

Vertically Mounted
Miniature Greenhouse

Recycle wine boxes into a useful little space-saving greenhouse, which makes a handsome feature on a wall and gives you the chance to grow your own plants from seed, with some protection.

TIME IT RIGHT You can make this project at any time of the year but it's great to have it ready in early spring for seedlings or in fall to protect smaller plants through the winter.

1 Take an empty wine box and apply outdoor adhesive down one of the long sides. Place the second box on top and use clamps to hold in place until dry.

2 Screw the boxes together with two screws at either end of the central shelf, screwing diagonally so that they penetrate through to the sides for a stronger fix.

Project Steps

3 With a handsaw, cut out one of the long sides of the boxes; this will be the top of the greenhouse. Use this spare piece as a shelf and template for cutting further shelves.

4 Cut a piece of batten to fit the gap. Place it flush along the front edge, thin side facing out, and screw in place from the sides. This will be the top of the greenhouse; a lid will be fitted in its place that can be propped open.

5 Cut another piece the same size for the back of the gap, this time with the thick side facing out, and screw it in place.

6 Fit another piece of batten on the front edge of the bottom shelf, thick side facing out, to form a lip for the bottom of the greenhouse.

7 To make additional shelves, first measure and mark guidelines for where you would like the top edge to rest, bearing in mind the size of seedling pots and the height of seedlings.

8 Cut short pieces of batten for the shelves to rest on and screw them in position so that the top edges are level with the pencil guidelines.

9 Make the door frame from the architrave. To achieve a 45° miter joint in each corner, first position one piece on the corner of the box flush with the sides and draw a diagonal guideline.

10 Cut out and use as a guide for cutting the second piece of the joint, but draw the line on the reverse of the architrave. Repeat for each corner.

11 Glue and screw together the mitered sections. Use thinner screws and insert at an angle to pass through both pieces. Cut a piece of wood for the lid that will be slightly wider and deeper than the greenhouse when the door is in place. Attach to the back with two hinges, one near each end. Paint the box and door frame and leave to dry. You could also apply a coat of marine varnish for extra protection.

Project Steps

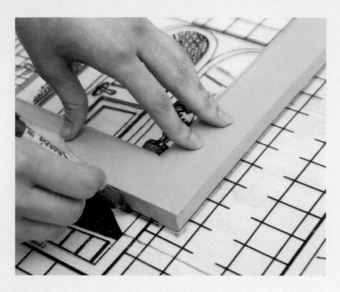

RECESSING SCREWS

Recess screws for a neater finish. After making the pilot hole with the correct size of drill bit for the screw, change to a thicker, short drill bit to create a small recess. Once the screw is in, fill with wood filler and sand when dry.

12 For the window, measure a piece of acrylic glass to cover the entire door frame. Cut out carefully with a handsaw and fix it to the back of the frame using silicone glue. Fix two hinges at either end of one of the long sides on the back of the door frame.

13 For the pilot holes, use a drill bit slightly wider than the screws for the acrylic, then switch to the correct size for the wood. Fix a door knob to the front.

14 Hang the greenhouse body. Fix lengths of batten to the back horizontally near the top and bottom. Screw 2 mirror fixing plates on either side of the battens and securely attach the greenhouse to your fence or wall. Additional support from a screw anchor may be required, depending on the surface. Finally, attach the door frame to the front and add a couple of small door hooks to keep it shut.

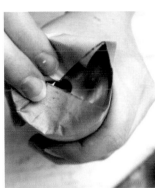

15 To make seed pots, cut strips of newspaper 30cm (12in) by 13cm (5in). Lay the aerosol can at the edge of a strip, 5cm (2in) in from the bottom. Roll and wrap the paper around the can to form a tube. Tuck the loose paper into the base.

16 Remove the pot, then fold in the top edge for strength and a neater finish. Pots will biodegrade, so place them straight into the ground when the plants are ready and all risk of frost has passed.

Care Advice

Where to site Choose somewhere which has sunlight for most of the day. You can add some shade for part of the day in summer if the sun is too strong.

Ventilation Air circulation is crucial for pest and disease control. Keep the door open for part of the day in spring, summer, and autumn, depending on the weather, closing it at night if temperatures are cooler. Prop the flap at the top of the greenhouse open with wooden blocks for extra ventilation in warm weather or minimal ventilation in cooler weather. In harsh winter conditions you may need some extra protection for the greenhouse such as bubble wrap around the outside.

TOOLS & EQUIPMENT

bamboo poles

exterior wood paint & paintbrush

large rectangular planting trough
  with drainage holes

tape measure

handsaw or lopper

green garden wire

wire cutters

gravel or crocks

multipurpose potting mix

garden twine

scissors

watering can

PLANT LIST

butternut squash

lemon squash

Rudbeckia laciniata 'Herbstsonne'

Thunbergia alata 'Lemon Star'

Funky Abstract

Bamboo Trellis

Get creative with bamboo poles. Make your own abstract-design trellis and use it to support climbing plants. This contemporary feature also makes an artsy screen for a small space.

 TIME IT RIGHT You can grow trailing squash plants vertically—it's a good use of space. Put squash plants in during early summer when the danger of frost is over; the other plants can go in at the same time.

1 Paint the bamboo poles with exterior wood paint; we chose black gloss for a bold, modern look that would contrast strongly with the plants. Leave to dry completely.

2 Start with two long upright poles positioned at either end of the trough. Measure the distance between them and cut two poles to size with a good overlap.

Project Steps

4 Add a long pole running diagonally across the base frame from bottom left to top right, tying securely with garden wire as before.

3 Tie these shorter poles at right angles to the uprights, one near the top and one in the middle. Do this securely by wrapping green garden wire several times around the pole intersections, then twist the ends together and cut off any excess wire.

5 Add poles of various lengths, attaching them to the frame at different angles; allow overlap and create abstract shapes, keeping the design asymmetrical. Paint the garden wire to match the poles and leave to dry.

6 To plant, add a layer of gravel or crocks to the base of the trough for drainage, then fill about two-thirds with multipurpose potting mix. Remove plants from their pots and position them in the trough, digging planting holes if they sit too high, then fill around with more potting mix and firm in. Water thoroughly.

PLANTING TIPS

Try climbing green beans as an alternative to squash. Green bean pods can be green, yellow, purple, or mottled deep pink and cream, and will also provide an appealing contrast to the background color of the bamboo poles.

7 As the plants start to put out climbing tendrils, give them a helping hand by lightly tying them onto the poles with garden twine.

Care Advice

Watering Containers above ground level are more exposed, so water often in the growing season, especially if hot and sunny, and while plants are establishing.

Feeding Add diluted liquid fertilizer to the water monthly in the main growing season. Squash needs more fertilizer than the other plants for fruit production; try misting them with diluted fertilizer as well, but not when in direct hot sunlight or the leaves might scorch.

General care Remove damaged foliage in the growing period. Some plants are not frost hardy and will die back if left outside in winter. Reduce watering in winter to minimal. Top off or change the potting mix in spring.

Squash needs plenty of water and fertilizer to produce a good, tasty crop.

Bean Feast

Nutritious, fast growing, and with attractive flowers and lush foliage, climbing beans are easy to grow from seeds and perfect for planting in pots for an edible container garden or to decorate an entrance.

TIME IT RIGHT Sow seeds indoors from mid-spring or outdoors in late spring. Beans are frost sensitive so only plant outside once all frost is past. You can expect to be harvesting 3 months after sowing.

TOOLS & EQUIPMENT

small pots with drainage holes

multipurpose potting mix

large containers with drainage holes

gravel or crocks, for drainage

general-purpose fertilizer

tall bamboo poles

garden twine

scissors

PLANT LIST

climbing green bean 'Pencil Pod Black Wax'

Italian climbing bean 'Borlotto Lingua di Fuoco'

runner bean 'Enorma'

1 To get your beans off to an early start, sow seeds 2in (5cm) deep from mid-spring in individual containers filled with potting mix. Water well and keep them indoors or in a greenhouse (see pp. 132–37 for early sowing instructions). The seeds need warmth to germinate.

2 You need to acclimatize tender seedlings in late spring before planting out. Place in a sheltered spot outside for a while during the day, but bring inside at night.

Project Steps

3 When your beans are ready for planting out, take a large, deep container and add a layer of gravel or crocks to aid drainage, then fill with potting mix mixed with a little general-purpose fertilizer. Put tall bamboo poles all around the outside edge. Secure the canes together at the top with twine to make a tepee.

4 Water the beans well, remove from their pots, and place in planting holes at the base of each pole, one per pole. Fill in around, firm the soil mix, and water again.

5 Encourage your beans to climb up the bamboo by lightly tying stems to the poles. Once established, the plants will find their own way to grow up the poles.

Care Advice

Where to site Beans like a sunny but sheltered site, however they will also do well in partial shade.

Watering and feeding Beans need plenty of moisture to produce a good crop, so water them regularly and frequently, especially in warmer weather, and daily in very hot weather. Never let the potting mix dry out. They need lots of food, too. Add liquid fertilizer, such as tomato feed or kelp extract once a week when flowers appear.

General care Pinch off the growing tips of plants once they reach the top of the poles, since this encourages a larger yield and keeps the tops of the plants less congested. Pick beans every 2–3 days to encourage more pods to form.

Climbing green bean 'Pencil Pod Black Wax' is a dwarf variety, but still needs poles for extra support. Ideal for early sowing, this vigorous bean crops throughout the summer.

Italian climbing bean 'Borlotto Lingua di Fuoco' has attractive red-and-green striped pods. Beans can be picked young or left to dry and stored for later.

Runner bean 'Enorma' produces attractive red flowers followed by long, tasty pods throughout summer and into early fall.

TOOLS & EQUIPMENT

large terra-cotta pot & drip tray

small plastic container

PVA glue

measuring cup

paintbrushes

2 colors of paint, ideally made
  for exterior use

bamboo poles or long sticks

crocks or gravel

multipurpose potting mix

garden twine

scissors

PLANT LIST

grape 'Black Hamburgh'

Lonicera sempervirens

Brightly Painted

Terra-cotta Pot for Climbers

Create a vibrant and welcoming display of climbers by simply painting a terra-cotta pot in bright colors. We've used two colors here: a sunny yellow and a warm purple, with climbing poles in a soft gray.

TIME IT RIGHT You can paint your pot at any time of year, but in cold, wet, or freezing conditions, paint somewhere frost free and dry. Plant in early spring or fall so the plants can get established.

1 You need to seal your terra-cotta pot first since the container is porous. In a small plastic container, mix up a solution of PVA glue and water at a ratio of 1:10 and then brush it all over the pot. Leave to dry for a couple of hours or overnight. Once dry, paint the top section of the pot yellow (you may need to do two coats), including some of the inside to below soil level, and leave to dry for a few hours or overnight.

Project Steps

3 Paint the pot's saucer, too, and then paint your support sticks (we used four) in a complementary color. We used one coat of paint to let some of the stick show through for a more decorative look. Seal with the PVA and water mix, if needed.

2 Using the rim molding as a guide, carefully paint the darker color on the remainder of the pot. Add a second coat if required. If you are not using exterior paint, seal with a coat of the diluted PVA solution.

4 Cover the drainage hole with some crocks or gravel to stop potting mix from spilling out and to help with drainage for the plant.

5 Fill your container halfway with multipurpose mix, then position your climbing poles around the edge of the pot, making sure they are evenly spaced.

6 Before planting, tie your poles together with garden twine near the top to secure them in a sturdy position, then plant your grapevine.

7 Lightly tie the grape stems to the poles to encourage them to attach. Then plant the honeysuckle—this will wind itself around the poles but needs some help, so tie lightly, too.

 ## Care Advice

 Watering and feeding Water plants regularly from mid-spring to early fall, and frequently in hot, dry weather—twice a day if exceptionally warm. It's best to water in the evening and use a saucer underneath for extra moisture. Use liquid feed diluted in water every 2–3 weeks or put slow-release plant food tablets in the soil during the growing season. Do not water or feed from late fall to late winter. Never overwater.

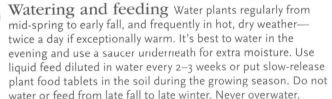 **General care** Keep your grapevine and honeysuckle contained by pruning above a bud in late winter, but remember that grapes have particular pruning requirements if you're aiming for a good crop. When pruning the honeysuckle, try to encourage branching for shape and flower production. You may need to repot both plants after a few years to a larger container.

Container care Keep sheltered during winter to protect it from frost. Clean the surface in spring with a damp cloth.

TOOLS & EQUIPMENT

old stepladder

tape measure & pencil

wooden batten

handsaw

bubble level

electric drill & drill bits

wood screws

sandpaper in a selection of grades

exterior wood paint & paintbrush

clear marine varnish (optional)

vintage wooden crates, galvanized
 metal tubs, terra-cotta pots

thick black plastic liner & scissors

PVA glue or staplegun

gravel or crocks

multipurpose potting mix

PLANT LIST

basil 'Purpleleaf'

carrot baby round 'Atlas'

chile pepper 'Medusa'

green onion 'Feast F1'

Helichrysum italicum

lamb's lettuce

Pelargonium sidoides

romaine lettuce 'Lonjoits Green',
 leaf 'Green Batavia' & 'Seurat',
 'Reine des Glaces'

Viola 'Blue Beacon', *cornuta*,
 'Trailing Lavender', 'Trailing Violet'

Upcycled
Stepladder Tiered Planter

Upcycle an old stepladder into a tiered planter by adding shelves across the steps. Paint in a snazzy color, plant in vintage crates, and, presto, you have an eye-catching, space-saving feature.

 TIME IT RIGHT You can paint your stepladder at any time of the year, but colder weather may slow drying time. Aim to plant containers with a mixture of seasonal plants and crops for year-round interest.

1 Take your stepladder and, starting at the second rung down from the top, measure and mark a piece of batten so that it will fit across the full width of the ladder inside the frame, directly opposite the rung. Cut the batten to size with a handsaw. Hold a bubble level against the top edge of the rung and mark this point on the opposite side of the frame.

Project Steps

2 Position the batten so the top edge is level with the mark just made, then screw to either side of the frame. This provides a second supporting rung for a planting shelf.

3 Measure and cut to size 4–5 battens to create a slatted shelf. They should extend 7¾in (20cm) beyond each rung with an extra 1¼–1½in (3–4cm) of excess wood on both sides; this excess will be cut off later for a finished look. Arrange the battens so that they are evenly spaced, then screw them in place to both rungs.

4 Once secured, measure and mark pencil guidelines along the battens at the point where they extend 7¾in (20cm) beyond each rung.

5 Cut along the guidelines to remove the excess wood, then sand the cut ends smooth. Repeat steps 1–5 to make further planting shelves. Position the shelves on alternate rungs to allow enough growing space for plants.

6 Paint the shelves and ladder with an exterior wood paint and leave to dry. If preferred, paint your tiered planter with a final coat of clear marine varnish for extra protection against the elements. The vintage crates would also benefit from a coat of varnish.

7 Drill drainage holes in the crates, if required, then line with black liner, glued or stapled to the base and sides. Cut a few holes in the base of the liner for drainage.

8 Add a thin drainage layer of gravel or crocks, then half-fill the crate with potting mix. Arrange your plants, fill around them with more soil mix, firm in, and water. If you are using galvanized buckets, there is no need to line them, but drill drainage holes if they don't have any.

Care Advice

Where to site Most plants need some sunlight, although many will grow in part shade. Put plants requiring more sun on the top rung or at the shelf ends.

Watering and feeding Water plants regularly during their growing season but less often during winter, depending on the plant's requirements. Add diluted liquid fertilizer to the water in the growing season but not in winter.

General care Move the crates often so each gets enough sunlight. Repot any plants that outgrow their containers. You could grow some vegetables as minis, planting them close together and harvesting when the crop is still small and tasty. Clean the ladder with a cloth after winter to keep it fresh and bright.

CONTAIN YOURSELF

TOOLS & EQUIPMENT

2 vintage galvanized steel tubs
 or buckets, one small enough to fit
 inside the other and leaving ample
 planting space

electric drill & metal drill bits

bricks

gravel or crocks

multipurpose potting mix

scissors

trowel

watering can

PLANT LIST

apple mint (*Mentha suaveolens*)

chocolate mint (*Mentha* x *piperata*
 f. *citrata* 'Chocolate')

cucamelon (*Melothria scabra*)

mint 'Hilary's Sweet Lemon'

strawberry 'Elan'

strawberry 'Rhapsody'

strawberry 'Eversweet'

Summer Drinks

Tiered Planter

Pick your own garnish for thirst-quenching drinks
while entertaining outdoors with this stylish tiered
planter filled with fruit, vegetables, and herbs
specially selected to complement summer drinks.

 TIME IT RIGHT Plant in early spring so everything
has time to grow and begin fruiting in time for summer.
You could also plant alternative garnishes such as a
small lemon tree, different herbs, and edible flowers.

1 If they don't already have them,
drill several drainage holes in
the bottom of each metal bath or
bucket using an electric drill fitted
with a metal drill bit.

2 Place the larger tub or bucket
in its final position. Stack
bricks in the center to create a
stable platform for the smaller tub
or bucket to set on.

Project Steps

3 Add a thin layer of gravel or crocks at the base of both containers for additional drainage and to ensure air can circulate around the roots of the plants, keeping them healthy.

4 Now add a layer of multipurpose potting mix, filling each container to about two-thirds full.

5 Position the smaller container on the raised platform, then start to plant them. Plant the lower tier with strawberries and mint, and the top tier with one or two cucamelon seedlings grown from seed (see General care).

6 Since mint grows vigorously and could otherwise crowd out the strawberries, restrict growth by keeping each plant in its plastic pot and simply cutting off the base.

7 Plant one side of the lower tier with mint and the other side with strawberries, leaving room for plants to spread. Make planting holes at a depth so the plants sit ¾–1¼in (2–3cm) below the rim of the bucket. Fill and firm in soil around the plants, then water thoroughly.

Care Advice

Where to site
The strawberries and cucamelon need good sun for crops to ripen, so place the planter in a sunny, sheltered site. Decide upon the final location before filling the planter because it will be heavy to lift.

Watering and feeding
Water often while plants are establishing and during the growing season. Add diluted liquid fertilizer 1–2 times a month in the growing season, but do not feed the mint or it may grow too much. Do not feed and reduce watering in winter.

General care
Remove any damaged, diseased, or dying foliage or fruit throughout the growing period. Keep mint plants in check by regular cropping and pruning back; remove plants if they get too big or invasive. Cut back strawberry plants after fruiting and plant any runners (plantlets at the end of an extended shoot) by pegging them in a separate pot then, once rooted, cutting them from the main plant. Sow cucamelon seeds indoors from early to mid-spring then plant out once danger of frost is over. Dig up the radishlike roots at the end of the season, cover lightly with potting mix and store in a cool, dry, frost-free place over winter; roots can be planted out again in mid-spring.

Try choosing strawberry varieties that fruit at different times in the growing season for a successional crop of fruit.

Harvest cucamelons, which have a fresh cucumber/melon/lime flavor, when the fruit are the size of grapes.

TOOLS & EQUIPMENT

wooden wine box or similar

electric drill & drill bits

slate roof tiles

white pencil or chalk

protective goggles

protective gloves

angle grinder

strong outdoor adhesive

black epoxy filler

paintbrush

matte black exterior paint

thick black plastic, for lining

scissors

metal skewer

Make-it-yourself

Slate Box Planter

Transform a wooden box into a stylish planter by enclosing it in slate. Inexpensive and easy to make, the planter can be filled with a range of plants—see pages 164–6 for an alpine-themed planting scheme.

 TIME IT RIGHT Constructing your planter should not take more than a couple of hours, but remember that you will need to leave it overnight and then allow for the paint to dry before you can fill it up.

1 Take your wooden wine box and drill drainage holes in the base using a large drill bit. You'll need several holes, so space them evenly across the base. Drainage is vital to prevent the plant roots from sitting in too much water and rotting.

Project Steps

2 Lay your tiles flat and, using a white pencil or chalk, draw around each side of the box, so you end up with 4 separate pieces marked out. Include an excess of ¾in (2cm) to the depth of each piece to provide a lip at the top of the planter.

3 Wearing protective goggles and gloves, carefully cut out the 4 slate pieces using an angle grinder. Make sure you do this on a stable surface that will not be damaged by the angle grinder.

4 Spread a layer of adhesive onto one outer panel of the box, then attach a matching slate piece and hold it in place until slightly bonded. Continue to attach the remaining slate pieces one by one. Wipe away any excess glue before it sets. Fill any gaps between the slate panels with black epoxy filler.

SELECTING SLATE

Reclaimed slate roofing tiles or slate offcuts are ideal for this project. Be sure they don't have any cracks in them or other damage. Clean up the surface with mild soap and water to bring out the natural patina of the slate.

5 Leave the slate-covered box overnight to allow the glue and filler to dry, then paint the base and the inside with black exterior paint; a matte paint blends better with the finish of the slate.

6 When the paint is dry, cut out some thick black plastic to fit the inside of the box and glue in place with adhesive. When the glue is dry, pierce some drainage holes in the base of the liner using a metal skewer.

TOOLS & EQUIPMENT

Slate Box Planter (see pp. 160–63)

gravel

soil-based potting mix

general-purpose fertilizer

large pieces of broken terra-cotta
   pots or similar

horticultural grit or aquarium gravel

PLANT LIST

Crassula 'Large Red'

Sedum oreganum

Sempervivum 'Kelly Jo'

Senecio 'Serpens'

Thymus 'Elfin'

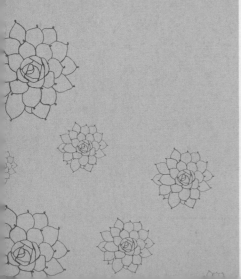

Rock Strata

Alpine Planter

Low-growing succulents and other alpines are perfect
for displaying in a box planter. This miniature alpine
landscape would make a stunning centerpiece for an
outdoor table and should be admired at eye level.

TIME IT RIGHT Early spring is the best time
to plant. You can also do this in summer, but it will
require more watering. The plants will offer color and
interest all year round.

1 Place a layer of gravel
over the base of the
box planter for drainage.
Succulents need good
drainage and do not like
to be sitting in water,
which will cause their
roots to rot. Add a layer
of gritty potting mix with
a little general-purpose
fertilizer added, filling to
halfway up the container.

 Project Steps

2 We used the broken rim of a terra-cotta chimney pot, or you can use large old plant pots, to create planting segments in the box for a natural landscape feature.

3 Lay out all your plants and roughly position them so you have a feel for how everything will look. Place taller plants at the back and lower, spreading ones at the front. Then take them out of their pots, gently teasing out any compacted roots, and start to plant up. Top off with a layer of soil mix.

Create a miniature alpine landscape for your planter by using broken terra-cotta pot rims or pieces of slate to simulate rock strata in a natural environment

PLANTING TIPS

Choose to put plants with different leaf textures and foliage colors next to each other to create interest and depth to the planting. Taller plants add different layers and height to the arrangement.

4 To finish off your alpine planter, dress with a layer of contrasting small grit, which helps to keep moisture in the soil and shows off the details of the plants.

Care Advice

Where to site Succulents need a sunny, warm site to thrive. They will need to be sheltered from the rain when left outside and protected from frost in winter. Bring inside during the dormant season and place on a sunny windowsill in a warm room.

Watering and feeding Water regularly in spring and summer, with just occasional watering in the fall. Do not water in winter and do not overwater at any time of year. Fertilizer added at planting time will keep plants fed for their first year and, after that, add a little diluted liquid feed to the water in spring and summer, but not in fall and winter.

General care Remove any spent flower stalks at the base of plants and remove any dead plant material before winter, since this attracts disease if left on during this period. Small scissors or pruners are useful for keeping plants pruned. Some plants will produce offsets, which can be snipped off and grown as cuttings; leave for 1–2 days to dry out and then pot in free-draining potting mix.

Put your alpine planter on a table to appreciate the textures and patterns of the plants. A gravel mulch shows off plants and helps to retain moisture.

TOOLS & EQUIPMENT

vintage metal containers in a range
of sizes

electric drill & metal drill bits

crocks or gravel

multipurpose potting mix

horticultural grit (for gooseberries)

trowel

slow-release fertilizer granules

wooden stakes & ties (optional)

watering can

gravel or well-rotted manure,
for mulch

netting, bamboo poles, & toppers

PLANT LIST

apple 'James Grieve', grown as
a vertical cordon

black currant 'Consort'

blueberry 'Bluecrop'

fig 'Brown Turkey', grown as a
half standard tree

golden marjoram

gooseberry 'Hinnomaki Red',
grown as a half standard shrub

sage 'Tricolor'

strawberry 'Eversweet'

Grow Your Own
Fruit in Tubs

You don't need a big garden to grow fruit trees and bushes—many can be grown in pots. As well as producing a crop, many fruit trees are ornamental, with pretty spring blossoms and fall leaf color.

TIME IT RIGHT You can plant container-grown fruit trees and bushes at any time of year, but be prepared to water frequently if planting in summer. Don't plant in freezing temperatures or severe weather.

1 Drill several drainage holes into the bottom of your container, if it does not have them already.

2 Place a layer of crocks (pieces of broken terra-cotta pots), gravel, or small pebbles in the base of the container, which will prevent the drainage holes from getting clogged up and ensure that air can circulate around the plant's roots.

Project Steps

3 Gooseberry bushes, shown being planted here, do not like to be waterlogged and will benefit from a relatively free-draining soil made of 2 parts potting mix to 1 part grit. Mix with a trowel before adding to the container. You can also mix some slow-release fertilizer granules into the mix.

4 Add the potting mix to the container, building up a base layer of soil to the correct height so that the top of the root ball will be 1¼–1½in (3–4cm) below the rim of the pot. Remove the bush from its container and tease out the roots, especially if it has become pot-bound and the roots have spiraled.

5 Position the plant in the container and fill in around it with your soil mix, keeping the bush level and centered as you do so. Add a stake to support a standard plant and tie it in if needed. Be sure to water the bush thoroughly after planting.

6 Add a 1¼in (3cm) layer of decorative gravel or another kind of mulch, such as well-rotted manure, which will help to retain moisture in the container.

7 Protect buds and fruit from hungry birds with netting draped around poles, using pole toppers, making sure none of the fruit presses against the mesh.

Care Advice

 ### Where to site
Fruit trees and bushes prefer growing in direct sun in a sheltered site. Turn pots regularly so that growth is balanced and the fruit ripens evenly. Some fruit may need their blooms protected from early frost, so cover with garden fabric or similar. Containers may need extra frost protection with bubble wrap in winter.

 ### Watering
Water regularly from spring to mid-fall, reducing to minimal levels in winter. Containers may need watering twice a day in summer. Water when the surface of the potting mix is dry and use a watering can with a long spout or hose to get water directly into the soil mix. Do not overwater and do not let the potting medium dry out completely. Place a container under the pot to catch excess water.

Feeding
Add diluted liquid fertilizer to the water monthly from spring to fall. Replace general feed with liquid tomato fertilizer weekly from mid-spring until late summer to encourage formation of fruit, then change back to general-purpose fertilizer from late summer to early fall and from early to mid-spring. Do not feed when plants are dormant in late fall and winter. Alternatively, you can add a controlled-release fertilizer tablet to the potting mix in early spring, although additional tomato feed is also beneficial.

 ### General care
Keep the pots free of weeds and add an annual mulch in early spring of well-rotted manure, leaf mold, or garden compost after watering containers thoroughly. Remove any dead, diseased, or dying foliage during the growing season. Prune mostly when plants are dormant and repot larger specimens every 2–3 years.

An elegant and space-saving method of growing fruit trees is to train them into an espalier (right). Formed around a single verticle stem, pairs of lateral shoots are pruned and trained along poles at 45° to the main stem in the first year, and then at right angles in the second year, when a second tier is added. Several tiers can be formed this way, growing flat against a wall to make the most of your small spaces.

Specific Fruit Advice

Black currants
Prune from leaf drop until winter, removing to ground level all weak, damaged, or diseased growth and a third of older growth to thin the bush and promote good air circulation.

Blueberries
Use acidic potting mix because blueberries prefer acidic soil. Keep the mix moist, and water with rainwater. Use fertilizer for acid-loving plants. Prune like black currants. Move to a sheltered, less frosty place in winter.

Figs
Prune in spring and regularly pinch off the growing point of the sideshoots to encourage fruit. Bring the pot into a frost-free place for winter, or wrap in plastic bubble wrap and garden fabric, then place in a sheltered place.

Gooseberries
Prune in summer by cutting back new growth to five leaves, then remove congested branches in winter to create better air circulation.

Strawberries
Place containers off the ground for better air circulation. Pot runners in late summer.

Apples
Choose plants grown on dwarf rootstock: M27 is the most popular variety. Single, slender cordons have fruit along the length of a vertical stem and are perfect for smaller spaces and containers, and only require light pruning each year in summer.

Fruit Gallery

Fruit trees in containers can be moved around so that the plant gets the best site and sunniest exposure. Cordons, espaliers, and fan-trained fruit trees are particularly good for smaller spaces; they give a high crop yield and are very attractive.

Grow herbs under fruit trees and bushes to maximize space. Remember to feed plants regularly. Also shown here: strawberries and blueberries.

Pictured above: black currants, gooseberries, and apples.

TOOLS & EQUIPMENT

safety equipment: surgical or rubber gloves and face mask—these are essential because cement can cause burns

2 metal or plastic bowls that will comfortably fit inside each other to give a reasonable rim width

concrete mix of white cement, silver sand, Portland or marble dust, and water; see steps 1 and 2 for calculating quantities

metric scales for weighing

large plastic bucket

measuring cup

dishwashing liquid (optional)

cork stoppers, cut to the correct depth for the base of your bowl

PVA glue

cooking oil & brush

additional sand or weights, to hold the top mold in place

sheet of plastic wrap, large enough to enclose the mold

metal file and/or sandpaper in various grades

PLANT LIST

Calluna vulgaris 'Elegantissima'

Make-it-yourself Concrete Planters

Sleek White Bowl

Making your own concrete planters is quick, inexpensive, and surprisingly easy—give it a try! This stylish white bowl will add a lovely contemporary feel to your planting.

TIME IT RIGHT The bowl takes one hour to make and 48 hours to harden. Make it under cover on a rainy day. Don't expose the hardening concrete to freezing temperatures—this could cause the water in the mixture to freeze and expand, cracking the concrete.

1 Use a pair of bowls, one fitting inside the other. Use plastic or metal mixing bowls, ice cream tubs, other food containers, etc.; note that bowls with an undercut or fluting in the wrong direction may be difficult to remove from the cast concrete. Carry out a water displacement test to calculate the quantity of dry mix: fill the outer mold with water, place the inner mold on top and press down gently, displacing water till the rims are level. Measure the volume remaining in milliliters; the total weight in grams of dry mix will be double that figure.

Project Steps

2 Concrete is a mix of cement, sand, and water added together in different quantities. A recommended ratio of cement to sand is 1:3. For a finer finish, stone dust can be combined with the sand at a 1:1 ratio. For the bowls we used, the volume of displaced water came to 2 liters, giving a total weight of 4kg dry ingredients, and because we used stone dust this broke down as 1kg cement, 1.5kg stone dust, and 1.5kg sand.

3 Wearing gloves and a face mask to protect against the caustic cement, measure out the dry ingredients and mix them together in a large plastic bucket until evenly combined.

4 The volume of water in milliliters needed will be 50–60% of the total weight in grams of cement. Our bowl required 1kg cement and 500–600ml water. Less water makes for stronger concrete but results in a more solid mix that can be more difficult to work with.

5 If you like, add of squirt of dishwashing liquid, which will act as a plasticizer to make the concrete more malleable. Mix until there are no streaks of dry ingredients and the concrete forms firm, doughlike clumps.

6 Glue a cork stopper in the center of the larger mold; this will create a drainage hole. Oil the bowl and cork to aid removal. Line the mold with concrete, pressing down with your knuckles and spreading it up the sides to start to create the bowl shape. Build up evenly until level with the top of the cork.

7 Oil the base (and lip, if it has one) of the inner mold and position in the center. Fill in between the molds until the concrete is level with the top. You may need to keep pressing down on the inner mold to ensure it sits on the cork, especially if the concrete starts to become more liquid.

8 Add sand or weights to hold down the inner mold and gently tap the sides of the outer mold to level the surface and release air bubbles. Place on a flat surface, wrap loosely in plastic, and keep out of direct sunlight so it does not harden too quickly. Leave for 24–48 hours. Remove the inner bowl and cork, then turn upside down to remove the outer bowl. Pouring boiling water on metallic molds will help to release them.

9 Smooth any sharp edges with a metal file and finish off the surface with sandpaper, working from rough to fine grades of paper, as desired.

Make-it-yourself Concrete Planters

Carnivorous Garden

With their exotic and unusual appearance, and fascinating ability to obtain their nutrient needs by trapping and feeding on insects, carnivorous plants make a bold impact. They are also surprisingly easy to look after, once you understand their needs.

TIME IT RIGHT Plant mid-spring to summer to enjoy the carnivorous plants at their peak of interest. They will die back in winter, then start growing again in spring. If possible, allow one week for the potting mix to reach correct acidity before planting.

TOOLS & EQUIPMENT

wide, relatively shallow concrete
planter, made from instructions
pages 176–9; we used two large
bowls for the molds

gravel (optional)

organic coir mixed with perlite 3:1
(see step 3)

trowel

rainwater or distilled water

watering can

PLANT LIST

Darlingtonia californica

Dionaea muscipula

Drosera capensis

Sarracenia flava

Sarracenia 'Juthatip Soper'

Sarracenia moorei (*flava* x
leucophylla)

Sarracenia purpurea subsp.
purpurea

sphagnum moss (optional; if dried,
soak for at least 1 hour and squeeze
out excess water before using)

Project Steps

1 Clean the container before
planting to remove any residue
and particles that may harm the
plants. Plan your arrangement:
place delicate, low-growing plants
at the front where they can be
appreciated, then continue
building up the layers, putting
taller plants at the back. Aim
for a natural look that shows off
each individual variety of plant.

2 Since our concrete planter was
made without a hole in the
base, we added a very thin layer
of gravel for drainage. This is
not essential, however, and it is
important to leave space so the
potting mix layer is deep enough
to allow water to get under the
roots of the plants.

3 Fill with a growing medium
of three parts organic coir to
one part perlite. Carnivorous plants
need slightly acidic, nutrient-poor
soil, and the correct potting mix is
essential for plants to thrive. You
can replicate this with the organic
coir and perlite mix, but check
labels carefully on the coir mix
to ensure they don't contain any
salt or added nutrients, which are
likely to kill the plants.

4 Water the potting mix with rainwater or distilled water, and ideally leave for a week to allow the soil to reach optimum acidity. Never use tap water since carnivorous plants like acidic, nutrient-poor conditions and tap water is generally too alkaline with too many mineral nutrients.

5 Remove plants from pots and place them in their planting locations, making sure you leave room for plants to grow and expand without crowding each other. Plant so that the crowns of plants are just below the soil surface.

6 Water the plants well. They like to have damp conditions and a little water but not a huge amount, similar to a bog garden environment, so keep the medium moister than for other plants. Add a water-retaining mulch of sphagnum moss if you like. In time, moss will also grow naturally on the surface.

Care Advice

Where to site Keep in a sunny spot but not one with scorching hot summer sun. Protect from frost by bringing them into a more sheltered spot like a porch or shed in winter.

Watering Keep water levels topped up and never let the potting mix dry out. When watering, water at the base of plants directly into the soil, so as not to wash off any sticky coating that plants have or cause stress, e.g. flytraps can close in alarm if watered from above. Make sure any pitchers on plants have a little water in them, too. Reduce watering in winter when plants are dormant, but still keep the surface slightly damp.

Carnivorous plants thrive on poor, nutrient-free soil, and you should not need to feed them since they get all their nutrients from insects they catch.

General care Remove any dead foliage and pitchers to keep plants neat. The foliage will die down in the winter when plants are dormant but leave this on until late winter/early spring for added protection, removing old foliage at the base of the plants as new buds and tips emerge. Move the container to a less sunny but cool location while plants are dormant, where it will be protected from heavy frost and winter conditions. Wrap the container in bubble wrap and cover with garden fabric for added protection if winters are very harsh.

Make-it-yourself Concrete Planters

Slate-gray Window Box

The color of this elegant window box planter was created by mixing black pigment with the cement. Experiment by adding different colored pigments to the mix to create a unique work of art for your windowsill.

TIME IT RIGHT This project involves more effort than some others but is well worth it. Allow one day to construct the mold and cast the concrete, and 48 hours for the concrete to cure. Make under cover if raining and protect the curing concrete from freezing temperatures.

Size Matters

Concrete may crack without reinforcement if the edge width is too narrow for its size. Our box edges were 1in (2.5cm) wide; for boxes larger than the one in this project, include reinforcing mesh or rods in the construction. Melamine-faced particle board makes a good mold: its surface aids unmolding. Particle board or plywood must be sealed with 2–3 coats of shellac.

Adapt the size of the planter to suit your space but consider the weight of the concrete.

TOOLS & EQUIPMENT

½in (1.5cm) or thinner melamine-
  coated particle board (see page 184)

wooden batten

tape measure & pen or pencil

handsaw

PVA glue & clamps

electric screwdriver & screws

safety equipment: surgical or
  rubber gloves & face mask

concrete mix of 4.25kg white or
  grey cement, 425g black pigment
  powder, 6.38kg silver sand,
  6.38kg stone dust, and 2.125l water

metric scales for weighing

plastic buckets, bowls, & strainer

measuring cup

dishwashing liquid (optional)

cork stoppers

cooking oil & paintbrush

trowel or metal scraper

sheet of plastic wrap, large
  enough to enclose the mold

metal file &/or sandpaper in
  various grades

PLANT LIST

Agapanthus dwarf varieties, such as
  'Peter Pan' or 'Blue Baby'

Project Steps

1 Calculate and measure the pieces for the outer mold to achieve your desired box size, remembering battens are attached on the outside. Internal dimensions for our box were 8 x 7.5 x 7.5in (46 x 19 x 19cm). Using a handsaw, cut the pieces accurately to size; or you could opt to get them machine cut at a building supply store.

2 Calculate the size of the inner mold to give a suitable width to base and sides of the box (see p.184), and cut pieces to size; ours measured 16 x 5½ x 8¼in (41 x 14 x 16.5cm). Note that battens are fixed to the inside and there is no base piece. When constructing the molds, first glue the batten to the boards with PVA glue, clamp together, and leave for one hour before screwing it all together.

3 Measure out the concrete mix, adapting the quantities listed in proportion to the size of your box (see also page 178). To color it, add pigment up to 10% of the weight of the cement; any more than 10% will weaken the structure. Sift together the cement and pigment to ensure even distribution of color. Mix in the remaining dry ingredients. Add water, erring on a solid mix, and a squirt of dishwashing liquid to aid plasticity, if you like.

4 Cut several corks for drainage holes to the correct depth, space evenly, and glue in place. Brush oil over the corks and base and sides. Build a base layer of concrete level with the tops of the corks. Use a trowel or scraper to spread, pack in, and smooth the concrete.

5 Rest the inner mold on the base layer. Pack concrete into the cavity between the molds to build up the sides. As you fill, check that you're maintaining consistent width all around by using spacers.

6 Once you have filled the mold, tap all around to help remove air bubbles and then smooth the top edge of the concrete with a trowel. Loosely cover the mold with a sheet of plastic and leave to harden on a level surface, out of direct sunlight, for 48 hours.

7 Remove the inner mold by unscrewing the batten and then easing out the pieces of particle board. Disassemble and remove the outer mold and then remove the corks. Finish off by smoothing rough edges with a metal file or grades of sandpaper.

Why not try…

Make concrete containers in different sizes, shapes, and colors, and group together for a feature effect. Great for small spaces like the tops of walls, steps, shelves, and corners.

PLANTING TIPS

Create a changing display of plants for year-round interest. Partner permanent evergreen plants, such as ivy, which give structure, with seasonal plants for interest at different times of the year. Candles create an ambient nighttime display.

Two Ways to

Decorate Your Terra-cotta Pots

Readily available and inexpensive, terra-cotta flowerpots are perfect for decorating with paint, decoupage, and other craft materials. Group your decorated pots together for a stylish effect and to show off your creativity.

 TIME IT RIGHT You can create your decorated pots all year round, but prepare them under cover if the weather is harsh or wet. Paint and glue may not dry properly in freezing conditions. As well as plants, you can fill your pots with other items; try pinecones for a festive look in December.

Decorated pots look great when grouped together. The plants we used here (from left to right) are: *Cynara cardunculus*, *Echeveria* sp., *Laurus nobilis*, *Echinacea purpurea* 'White Swan', *Thymus* × *citriodorus* 'Argenteus', *Helichrysum italicum*, *Sedum spectabile* 'Autumn Joy'.

TOOLS & EQUIPMENT

terra-cotta pots—these can be sealed
first with a 1:10 solution of PVA
glue and water; leave to dry for
a couple of hours or overnight
before painting

acrylic or exterior paint

paintbrushes

sandpaper in various grades

decoupage material: choose prints
and photos cut from wallpaper,
wrapping paper, magazines, paper
napkins, newspapers

scissors

PVA glue

small paintbrush or glue spreader

clear marine varnish

PLANT LIST

Helichrysum italicum

Sedum spectabile 'Autumn Joy'

Project Steps

1 Paint the pot outside and
halfway down the inside, then
leave to dry. Lightly sand all over,
but sand more at the rim and base,
taking off a little of the paint along
the edges for an aged effect.

3 Turn your decoupage pieces
over to the nonpatterned side
and apply a thin covering of PVA
glue with a paintbrush or glue
spreader. Stick the pieces onto the
sides of the pots until you have
created a pleasing design all the
way around. Leave to dry.

2 Take one of your decoupage
sample pieces and carefully
cut around the outline with
scissors. We used floral and leaf
motifs cut from wallpaper.

4 Finally, brush over a thin layer
of clear marine varnish to
protect the decoration from the
elements and also to add a further
vintage look to the design. When
dry, plant your decorated pot.

Wallpaper is a good source for decoupage material, and
floral designs complement the planting arrangement.

TOOLS & EQUIPMENT

terra-cotta pots—these can be sealed
   first with a 1:10 solution of PVA
   glue and water; leave to dry for
   a couple of hours or overnight
   before painting

blackboard paint

paintbrushes

acrylic or exterior paint

sandpaper in various grades

clear marine varnish

white chalk

cloth

PLANT LIST

Echeveria sp.

Laurus nobilis

Project Steps

1 Paint blackboard paint around
   the sides of the pot but not the
rim. Leave to dry.

2 Paint the rim of the pot and
   halfway down the inside in an
attractive contrasting color. Leave
to dry, then lightly sand areas of
the rim for a weathered look.

3 Paint clear marine varnish over
   the rim area only for extra
protection. Rub white chalk all
over the blackboard paint, creating
an even, fairly solid covering.

4 Take a dry cloth and rub off
   most of the chalk so that the
pot is left with an appealing
slate-colored tinge. This also cures
the blackboard paint, which is
necessary if you wish to write
on the pot, otherwise the writing
will be unreadable.

These slate-effect pots looks stylish left just as they are, but you may find it a useful and attractive addition to write the plant's name and care instructions on the pot in chalk.

GO WILD

TOOLS & EQUIPMENT

single-bottle wooden wine box with slide-out lid, plus the lid from a second box or equivalent

paint brushes & exterior paint

marine varnish (optional)

metal ruler & square

pencil

small handsaw

strong outdoor adhesive

pond liner or similar

utility knife

capillary matting

scissors

nails & sturdy brass picture hook

hammer

soil-based potting mix mixed 3:1 with horticultural grit

garden wire

wire cutters

FOR THE INSECT ROOMS

bamboo poles & pruning shears

small logs & electric drill & drill bits

bark & sticks

pinecones

corrugated cardboard

terra-cotta pots

woodland moss

PLANT LIST

Jovibarba hirta

Sedum album

Sedum dasyphyllum

Sedum hirsutum

Sedum sexangulare

Sedum spurium 'Variegatum'

Sempervivum arachnoideum 'Hookeri'

Portable Hanging

Insect House with Green Roof

With its living succulent roof, this attractive insect house has lots of different rooms to encourage helpful, beneficial insects likes bees, ladybugs, and lacewings to seek shelter in your garden.

TIME IT RIGHT Make your insect house from spring to early fall, when the plants for the green roof will be actively growing so they can root in, and before insects start looking for places to hibernate.

1 The insect house is made out of a single-bottle wooden wine box. Remove the lid and then paint the box; you could also apply marine varnish to protect it further.

2 Take the lid and measure 2 roof pieces 8in (20cm) long. Divide the rest in half diagonally to form 2 triangular pieces for the sides. Cut out with a handsaw.

Project Steps

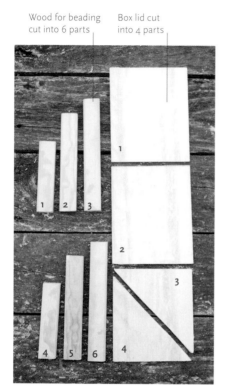

Wood for beading cut into 6 parts

Box lid cut into 4 parts

3 Measure and cut out 6 pieces of beading from the second lid (or equivalent): 2 long, 2 medium, 2 short. These will form an edge around the roof for planting space.

4 Glue the main roof pieces in a pitched shape using a strong outdoor adhesive. Glue on the triangular side pieces flush with the roof edge. Glue the beading around the edges. Paint the roof and leave to dry. Apply a layer of marine varnish, if using.

5 To provide waterproofing for the green roof, line it with some pond liner (you could also use a heavy-duty black garbage bag). Using a sharp utility knife, cut it so that it lines the exposed roof and also comes up the sides of the beading, then trim off any excess and glue in place.

6 Now add a piece of capillary matting on top. This provides wicking for the plants, holding moisture so that the water doesn't all run off. Cut the matting to size with scissors; it doesn't need to cover the beading.

7 Nail a brass picture hook near the top of the box with a hammer. Glue the roof in place with strong outdoor adhesive.

8 Collect items for the insect rooms. Cut pieces of bamboo pole to the depth of the box with pruning shears and drill holes into the end of a log to create homes for solitary bees. Bark, pinecones, and sticks provide habitats for beetles, centipedes, ladybugs, spiders, and pill bugs. Rolled up corrugated cardboard or stacked terra-cotta pots are ideal homes for pill bugs.

Little crevices are perfect places for insects to hibernate

Project Steps

9 Build up different layers of insect rooms to create your "hotel", filling any larger gaps with moss.

10 For the green roof, remove plants from their pots, cut off the root ball to match the beading depth, and place snugly in the planting space, filling any gaps with a mixture of potting mix and grit. Thread wire through the picture hook and hang outside.

Care Advice

General care The green roof doesn't need watering, apart from occasionally at the start while plants are establishing, and doesn't need feeding; it will grow quite well without too much attention. Just cut off spent flower stalks and dead leaves every now and then. You can leave your insect house outside all year round, but if the winter is very wet, move it somewhere more sheltered from downpours. Leave the insect rooms to settle and be inhabited by your beneficial friends, adding more materials occasionally as needed.

TOOLS & EQUIPMENT

drawer from an old chest of drawers

exterior wood paint & paintbrushes

clear marine varnish (optional)

electric drill with wood drill bits

scissors, thick black plastic, and glue

gravel

seed potting mix

large scoop or trowel

small folding table (optional)

PLANT LIST

alpine scabiosa

anise hyssop

betony

carpet moss

corncockle

crested dog's tail

greater knapweed

harebell

lady's bedstraw

oxeye daisy

small scabiosa

sweet marjoram

Verbascum speciosum

wild marjoram

Vintage Drawer

Wildflower Meadow

Create your own patch of wildflower meadow in an old vintage drawer. Your wildlife haven will attract lots of beneficial insects and is both simple to make and easy to maintain.

 TIME IT RIGHT Plant in early spring so that insects coming out of hibernation have an early nectar source. If you want to grow wildflowers from seed, sow these in either early spring or early fall.

1 Paint your drawer with exterior paint and finish with a coat of marine varnish for extra protection, if you like. We painted our drawer to contrast with our display table.

2 Drill several drainage holes in the base of the planter, spacing them evenly across the area.

Project Steps

3 Cut to shape some thick black plastic to line the drawer, which will protect the wood and prevent it from rotting. Glue the liner into place around the sides.

4 Cut drainage holes in the base of the liner. Next, put a thin layer of gravel over the base of the plastic, which will also help with drainage.

5 Add seed mix and fill to about two-thirds of the height of the plastic liner. It is important to use seed mix—multipurpose mix is too rich in nutrients.

6 Plan your arrangement before planting, seeing which plants fit best together. Aim for a natural look that is not too controlled.

7 Start to plant your drawer. Gently tease any pot-bound roots to give them a good start. Fill any gaps between plants with soil mix.

Project Steps

8 Water your wildflower arrangement well and finish by mulching with carpet moss for decoration and to keep in moisture. Display the meadow on a small folding table, where the plants can be admired and enjoyed up close.

Care Advice

 Where to site You will need to keep your meadow outdoors in a sunny or shady location, depending on the plants chosen. Perennial plants do not need protection from frost and harsh weather, but annual wildflowers will need to be sown or planted each spring.

 Watering Water regularly from spring to mid-fall, reducing to a minimum in winter. Do not overwater the container, nor let it dry out completely. You do not need to feed the meadow at any stage because wildflowers prefer soil low in nutrients.

General care Remove any dead, diseased, or dying foliage during the growing season, but leave seedheads on until early to mid-fall so that plants self-seed naturally. Thin out or repot any excess seedlings in mid-spring. You will need to cut every plant down to just above soil level in mid-fall so that stems and foliage are not left on over the winter. This will increase nutrient levels and therefore reduce the amount of flowering the following year.

For a smaller space or alternative wildflower meadow, plant a large metal garden sieve. Simply line (adding drainage holes if needed), cover the base with gravel, then add seed mix and plants.

TOOLS & EQUIPMENT

rubber or surgical gloves

wicker hamper

dishcloth or old rags

exterior paint & clear marine varnish

scissors, thick black plastic, and glue

gravel

multipurpose potting mix

PLANT LIST

Achillea 'Martina'

Agastache 'Black Adder'

Aster macrophyllus 'Twilight'

Centranthus ruber 'Coccineus'

Digitalis grandiflora

Echinacea purpurea 'Ruby Giant'

Echinops ritro 'Veitch's Blue'

Erigeron karvinskianus

Gaura lindheimeri

Helenium autumnale 'Sahin's Early Variety'

Lavandula x *intermedia* 'Grosso'

Linaria purpurea 'Canon Went'

Monarda 'Cambridge Scarlet'

Origanum laevigatum 'Hopleys'

Stipa tenuissima

Verbena bonariensis

Bee and Butterfly
Wildlife Hamper

Planted with nectar-rich plants, this hamper will keep bees and butterflies supplied with food. You'll enjoy watching the different species of beneficial insects that come and tuck into this fast-food feast.

TIME IT RIGHT Early spring is a good time to plant your hamper so that insects coming out of hibernation have an early food source. Add spring and fall bulbs to the planting to extend the season.

1 Wearing protective gloves, give the hamper a light paint wash by dipping a cloth or rag into paint and rubbing it all over the wicker. Leave to dry, then add a layer of marine varnish in the same way for extra weather protection.

2 Cut the plastic to line the hamper; this both protects and helps retain soil and moisture. Glue in place and, when dry, cut several holes in the liner for drainage.

Project Steps

3 Put a thin layer of gravel across the base of the plastic, which will help with drainage.

4 Add the potting mix and fill to about half the height of the plastic liner to leave room for the root balls of the plants.

5 Plan your planting arrangement, seeing which plants fit best together. Aim for a natural arrangement and place grasses between flowering plants to add texture and movement.

Bees prefer single flowers rather than double ones, while butterflies like small tubular flowers and those with a large central area

6 Plant your hamper, gently teasing out any pot-bound roots to help get them off to a good start. Fill any gaps between plants with potting mix and water thoroughly.

Care Advice

Where to site Place in a sheltered, sunny location (although some daytime shade is fine). The hamper is planted with outdoor perennials that do not need protection from frost and harsh weather.

Watering and feeding Water regularly from spring to mid-fall, reducing to minimal levels in winter. Do not overwater or let the potting mix dry out completely. Add diluted liquid feed to the water monthly from spring to fall.

General care Remove any dead or dying foliage during the growing season. You will need to cut every plant down to just above soil level in late winter or early spring. When the plants outgrow the hamper, split them into more plants and replant the hamper at the same time.

A watering can with a long spout gets water directly into the potting mix.

A bee enjoying *Agastache* 'Black Adder' (top).
Digitalis grandiflora, *Achillea* 'Martina', and *Verbena bonariensis* (center).
The large central cone of *Echinacea purpurea* 'Ruby Giant' is perfect for bees and butterflies (bottom).

TOOLS & EQUIPMENT

terra-cotta saucers

bamboo poles, cut to slightly
  different lengths

acrylic or exterior paint

paintbrushes

clear marine varnish (optional)

selection of large ceramic or enamel
  cups, mugs, and small bowls

masking tape

electric drill with ceramic and metal
  drill bits

exterior glue

pole toppers

bricks or large rocks (optional)

bird seed

Cup and Saucer

Bird Stations

Watching birds in your outdoor environment is both
fascinating and relaxing. Add a decorative touch
while looking after your feathered friends with these
delightful feeders made from cups, mugs, and bowls.

TIME IT RIGHT Make these feeders in time
for fall when birds need to find extra food supplies to
see them through the winter. Garden birds need to eat
all year round, however, so keep birdseed topped up.

1 Paint the saucers and
poles in a variety of
colors. Envision how they
will work with your cups
and bowls, when
choosing your colors,
and try matching or
contrasting the colors
of the saucers and poles.
Leave to dry and then
add a coat of marine
varnish, if you like, for
extra protection against
the elements.

Project Steps

2 Drill a hole in the base of each of your seed holders. This will help rainwater to drain away so that the birdseed doesn't get too waterlogged. Make a masking-tape cross where you want to drill for a clean finish and to prevent slipping.

3 Glue a pole topper onto one end of each bamboo pole and leave them to dry.

5 Apply several dabs of glue to the base of each cup or bowl and stick them in place on the saucers. Don't glue all the way around—this will allow water to drain out easily.

4 Apply glue to the tops of the pole toppers, then glue these to the middle of each of the painted terra-cotta saucers. Leave them to dry completely.

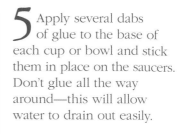

6 Insert the poles firmly into the ground. Support them with bricks or large rocks if they still feel a little loose.

 Project Steps

NO GARDEN?

If you don't have a patch of garden soil where you can insert your feeders, try putting them into a flowerpot instead. Simply place the pole with the feeder in the center of a pot, fill around with concrete, and leave it to dry.

7 Fill the cups with bird seed and the bowls with water. Keep both regularly replenished and watch the birds flock to your garden!

 ## Care Advice

 Where to site The ideal location for your bird feeders and bath is somewhere quiet so the birds won't be disturbed, relatively open and sunny so that they have a good field of vision, but also near a large shrub or other plants where they can hide from predators. Several feeding stations allow smaller birds lower down in the pecking order to grab a meal.

 General care Clean out feeders and remove any debris regularly, particularly after long spells of wet weather. Use a cloth to clean the inside of the feeder and water bowl. Change the water in the bowl frequently.

Seedcake Hangers for

Hungry Birds

1 Measure half the weight of fat to bird seed; use a hard fat such as suet, drippings, lard, or white vegetable fat. Melt the fat in a pan, stir in the seeds, then spread onto a baking tray to the same depth as the cutters. Cool slightly, then press cookie cutters into the mix.

2 Remove the filled cookie cutters and leave to set. To hang them, cut lengths of garden twine, make a hole at the top of each seedcake with a skewer, thread through and knot the twine.

Seedcakes are especially useful for garden birds in the lean winter months, when other food sources are scarce. Tie them directly on to a suitable support or use clothespins for easy removal when the seedcakes need replenishing.

PLANT PRACTICAL

Choosing Plants

For your plants to survive and flourish, it is vital to match the right plants to the right conditions, so make sure you know what your growing space is like before buying. Is it sheltered, damp, and shady... or exposed, dry, and sunny?

Practical considerations

Think about what you want to grow and how much time you have to look after your plants. Some plants need less attention than others, but all plants require some care. Consider the time of year for your flowering display, too. Some plants look good when in flower but don't add anything else for the rest of the year. Combine these with other plants whose flowers, stems, or foliage add interest across other seasons. Look for plants with a good shape that can be used as a focal point to anchor a changing display. Consider what containers you are going to use. All containers need drainage and should be easily accessible for watering and care. Consider too how they might affect the overall look of your planting. Complex arrangements work best in less ornate containers where the focus is on the planting itself. Quirky, unusual containers add an element of fun, so try anything suitable and adapt for drainage, if need be.

Be inspired

Seek inspiration for your garden style and explore planting ideas. Buy a big notebook and visit open gardens, jotting down what plants you like and different planting designs. Don't be afraid to ask questions of garden owners and gardeners, who will usually be more than happy to tell you more. Have a look through gardening books and seek out magazines for ideas, keeping a note of anything that appeals. Don't forget the great outdoors for inspiration! Nature has a clever way of arranging plants and landscape features that blend perfectly: wildflower meadows; prairies; seaside planting; fields; shady plants in woods; or streams and ponds.

Finding your style

Do you want the planting to be ornamental, or productive with herbs, vegetables, and fruit? Do you want to screen off neighboring buildings? Do you want year-round interest? What style of planting particularly appeals to you? Planting styles can be re-created in smaller spaces by careful plant selection, so take time to really know what you want to achieve if you are planning a major design in your gardening space. As well as your growing conditions, take into account your home and how your planting will blend in with the building. Some planting styles may suit your home more than others, but don't be afraid to try something unusual for a different approach. Most of all, enjoy creating a garden space that is unique to you and reflects your own style and personality.

Although there are notable exceptions, such as succulents, most plants in containers will need a lot of watering, so make sure you have time to do this and easy access to water.

If the growing conditions of light, temperature, and exposure allow it, almost any style of planting, such as this English garden feel, can be adapted to fit a smaller space.

What sort of plant?

Sometimes it's obvious what type of plant you need to buy, like a tree, but sometimes it isn't, and it's useful to know the difference between the groupings so you can choose the correct plant for your needs.

Annuals complete their life cycle in one growing season. They will germinate, flower, produce seeds, and die in one growing season. Examples include annual bedding plants such as geraniums, zinnias, marigolds, forget-me-nots, and sweet peas.

Perennials last more than three growing seasons, but the name is often used to cover herbaceous perennials, which are mostly border plants that survive year after year, with foliage usually dying back when the plant is dormant in winter. Examples include penstemons, asters, primroses, sedums, and hostas. Some perennials need a bit of protection from frost and extremely cold weather.

Bulbs are modified stems adapted to store food, and different bulbs can be planted in spring, summer, and fall for year-round successional interest.

Shrubs and trees are woody perennials that add structure to planting. Some plants are evergreen, but most lose their leaves when the plant goes dormant.

Grow your own

Growing plants from seed is cost effective and fun for the whole family. You'll need containers, seed potting mix, and somewhere light and warm to start them off (see pages 132–7).

Some seedlings, particularly annuals and vegetable plants, will need protection from frost before they can be planted out.

Plants for sun

Key to symbols: ◌ Drought tolerant ⬤ Water often ⬤ Keep constantly wet ☼ Grow in full sun ☀ Partial shade ☀ Full shade

Echinacea purpurea

Outstanding late-summer display of large flowers with a prominent central cone. Easy to grow. Attracts bees and butterflies. Seed heads look good in winter. Flowering time: July–September.

Care: Cut back to encourage flowers, but leave some seed heads over winter.

✿✿✿ ☼–☀ ⬤

Aster

Ranges from small alpine species to taller plants. Pretty daisylike flowers, in white, pink, lilac, or blue, bloom in late summer. Loved by bees and butterflies.

Care: Choose mildew-free varieties for best foliage. Cut back after flowering or leave until spring for winter interest.

✿✿✿ ☼ ⬤

Helenium autumnale

Upright plants with showy, daisylike flowers from late summer through fall. Rich flower colors range from buttery yellow to warm orange to bronzy red. The central cone is loved by bees.

Care: Deadhead, leaving some seed heads. Divide every 3–4 years.

✿✿✿ ☼ ⬤

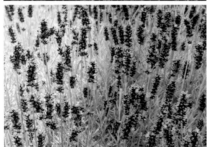

Lavandula angustifolia

Small shrubs with aromatic leaves and spikes of fragrant blue, purple, pink, or white flowers in summer. Can grow quite large and lose its shape, so choose shorter varieties for smaller spaces.

Care: Trim after flowering. Shape in spring. Don't cut into old woody growth.

✿✿✿ ☼ ◌

Sedum spectabile

Good for a dry, sunny spot. Late-summer flowers are adored by bees and butterflies, and fleshy leaves add interest year round. Some varieties have gray/green or purple/green foliage.

Care: Cut back after flowering or leave till spring for winter interest.

✿✿✿ ☼ ◌

Agapanthus

Excellent for containers. Upright funnel-shaped blue or white flowers create impact in summer and early fall. Attractive seed heads in winter. Choose perennial types.

Care: Feed regularly during growing season and keep soil mix moist.

✿✿✿–✿✿ ☼ ◌

See also... *Aeonium* p.228, *Agastache* p.230, Bronze fennel p.230, *Buddleia* p.230, *Calamagrostis* x *acutiflora* 'Karl Foerster' p.233, *Canna* p.231, *Dianthus alpinus* p.228, *Dipsacus fullonum* p.230, *Echeveria* p.228, *Phlox douglasii* p.228, *Rosa rugosa* p.229, *Sempervivum* p.228

Plants for shade and semishade

❋❋❋ Fully hardy ❋❋ Can survive outside in mild regions/sheltered sites ❋ Move inside for winter

Pulmonaria

Delicate blue, white, or pink flowers from late winter to early spring. Interesting blotchy leaves for most of the year. Lovely groundcover under other plants.

Care: Cut back old leaves before flowers appear, and again in summer.

❋❋❋ ☀–◐ 💧

Ferns

Ferns add architectural interest to displays, thrive in shady conditions, and come in a variety of heights and leaf shapes. Great to plant under taller plants. Some are evergreen.

Care: Incorporate organic matter in planting area. Keep soil moist.

❋❋❋ ☀–◐ 💧

Hosta

Easy to grow, hostas come in a wide range of heights and leaf colors, some with variegation. The perfect foliage plant for light to part shade, with pretty upright flowers in summer.

Care: Feed monthly during growing season with liquid or soluble fertilizer.

❋❋❋ ☀–◐ 💧

Bergenia

Evergreen perennial with dark green leaves, red tinted in winter, deep purple in some varieties. White or pink flowers in late winter and early spring. Easy to grow. Good groundcover plant.

Care: Remove faded flower spikes. Will grow in sun, but needs moist soil.

❋❋❋ ☀–◐ 💧

Astrantia major

Dainty pincushion-style flowers ranging from white or pale green to pinks and reds. Can also be planted in sun, but needs moist soil. Good to plant under taller plants to add layers.

Care: Deadhead, and cut back to soil level in fall or late winter.

❋❋❋ ◐ 💧

Helleborus

Hellebores' elegant flowers brighten up late winter days—they can be single or double, from pale pink to deep maroon. Large architectural leaves add interest.

Care: Cut back old foliage before flowers appear. Apply liquid or soluble fertilizer in fall and after flowering.

❋❋❋ ◐ 💧

See also... *Acer palmatum* p.231, *Buxus sempervirens* p.233, *Cornus* p.233, *Carpinus betulus* p.229, *Fothergilla major* p.231, *Hydrangea* p.233, *Photinia* p.229, *Taxus baccata* p.229, *Viburnum* x *bodnantense* p.233

Succulents, alpines, and air plants

Key to symbols: ◊ Drought tolerant   ◑ Water often   ● Keep constantly wet   ☼ Grow in full sun   ☀ Partial shade   ☀ Full shade

Sempervivum

Tight rosettes of fleshy leaves with upright flowers in summer. Foliage in shades of green, mahogany, bronzy purple, and crimson. Plant in a shallow container with free-draining soil mix.

Care: Repot when roots fill container. Do not overwater.

❇❇❇ ☼ ◊

Dianthus alpinus

Choose small alpine species with dainty and fragrant white or pink upright flowers in summer and evergreen foliage. Pretty in a tiny container. Use free-draining potting mix.

Care: Repot when roots fill container. Deadhead regularly. Do not overwater.

❇❇❇ ☼ ◊

Echeveria

Thick, fleshy leaves in rosettes, which can be green tinged with red autumnal hints, or dramatic black/purple. Clusters of upright flowers in spring. Looks good in traditional alpine pots.

Care: Not frost resistant so keep indoors in winter. Do not overwater.

❇ ☼ ◊

Phlox douglasii

Becomes a low-growing plant that will carpet shallow containers. Lilac, pale-blue, or pink flowers from late spring to early summer. Plant with free-draining potting mix.

Care: Repot when roots fill container. Deadhead regularly. Do not overwater.

❇❇❇ ☼–☀ ◊

Aeonium

Evergreen succulents. Rosettes of fleshy leaves. Star-shaped flowers in spring. Perfect for a sunny porch. Foliage is green with red tints in fall/winter. Blackish-purple varieties also available.

Care: Not frost resistant, so keep indoors in winter. Do not overwater.

❇ ☼ ◊

Tillandsia

Airplants don't need soil mix to grow; they absorb all their moisture and nutrients from the air. Versatile in a variety of arrangements, including growing on bark and shells or in sand.

Care: Mist regularly for humidity. Add liquid fertilizer in spring and summer.

❇ ☼ ◑

See also... *Aster* p.226, *Sedum spectabile* p.226

Plants for screening

✳✳✳ Fully hardy   ✳✳ Can survive outside in mild regions/sheltered sites   ✳ Move inside for winter

Phyllostachys nigra

An attractive, tall, upright bamboo with stunning blackish-brown stems. Wind rustling through leaves makes lovely sound. Plant in large containers. Under plant spring bulbs for seasonal colour.

Care: Remove older stems to thin out and show off newer stems.

✳✳✳ ☼–☼ ◖

Miscanthus sinensis

Ornamental grass with upright stems and arching silky flowers. Foliage has fall color or is evergreen. Good in containers and planted in groups.

Care: Leave flowers and stems over winter for added interest. Cut back to soil level in late winter.

✳✳✳ ☼–☼ ◖

Carpinus betulus

Hornbeam can be grown as a hedge in large containers. Foliage turns a rich yellow in fall. Plant retains leaves in winter, although it's not an evergreen.

Care: Keep containers well watered in growing season and feed monthly at the same time. Clip regularly for shape.

✳✳✳ ☼–☼ ◖

Rosa rugosa

Apple-green glossy foliage and single pink or white flowers in summer. Loved by bees. Huge red hips in fall. Good hedging plant and easy to grow.

Care: Leave rose hips for winter interest. Feed in growing season. Prune in late winter. Cut older wood to base.

✳✳✳ ☼ ◖

Taxus baccata

Slow-growing evergreen. Yew is easy to shape—it only needs cutting a couple of times each year. Make sure containers are large enough. Choose mature specimens for instant impact.

Care: Keep well watered and feed monthly in growing season.

✳✳✳ ☼–☼ ◖

Photinia

Evergreen shrubs with glossy leaves. Newer growth is bright red. Creamy white flowers in spring. You can clip the plants into a formal or informal hedge, or grow as standard shrubs.

Care: Keep well watered and feed monthly in growing season.

✳✳✳ ☼–☼ ◖

See also... *Buxus sempervirens* p.233, *Calamagrostis* x *acutiflora* 'Karl Foerster' p.233, *Cornus* p.233, *Euonymous* p.231, *Fatsia japonica* p.231, *Lonicera* p.230, *Pyracantha* p.233

Plants for wildlife

Buddleia

Known as the Butterfly Bush because the flowers, in shades of pink, mauve, blue, and white, provide a good source of nectar for butterflies. Some grow tall but can be kept smaller by pruning.

Care: Feed regularly in growing season. Prune each spring.

❄❄❄ ☼ ◐

Agastache

Aromatic leaves and upright spikes of blue, orange, or pink flowers. The small, tubular flowers invite bees and butterflies. Adds height to planting.

Care: Remove spent flower spikes throughout the season. Feed during the growing season.

❄❄❄ ☼ ◐

Dipsacus fullonum

The tall stems of teasel have conical seed heads lasting through winter that add interest and are good for birds. The pale-lilac flowers are adored by bees. Plants add a striking feature to displays.

Care: Leave seed heads over winter. Cut back to base in early spring.

❄❄❄ ☼–☀ ◐

Bronze fennel

Feathery bronze foliage with sulfur-yellow flat flowers in summer. Good seed heads for the birds in fall/winter. Tall, architectural shape with fragrant leaves. Looks good planted in gravel.

Care: Leave seed heads over winter. Cut back to base in early spring.

❄❄❄ ☼ ◊

Digitalis purpurea

Bees adore foxgloves! Flower colors on tall spikes range from traditional purple to white, apricot, and yellow. Although a woodland plant, some foxgloves enjoy sunny sites.

Care: Cut back spikes after flowering, but leave some to self-seed.

❄❄❄ ☀–❉ ◐

Lonicera

Honeysuckle is useful to grow up a trellis and as larger shrubs. Fragrant summer flowers are loved by bees and butterflies. Berries follow in fall. Birds like to nest in thicker areas.

Care: Prune for shape in early spring. Tie in stems. Feed in growing season.

❄❄❄ ☼–☀ ◐

See also... *Aster* p.226, *Calamagrostis* x *acutiflora* 'Karl Foerster' p.233, *Echinacea purpurea* p.226, *Helenium autumnale* p.226, *Iris versicolor* p.232, *Lavandula* p.226, *Pyracantha* p.233, *Rosa rugosa* p.229, *Sedum spectabile* p.226

Plants for foliage

❈❈❈ Fully hardy ❈❈ Can survive outside in mild regions/sheltered sites ❈ Move inside for winter

Heuchera

Slender stems have spikes of small bell-shaped flowers in late spring, and interesting, mostly evergreen foliage. Leaf colour ranges from pale bronze to green, and purple.

Care: Remove faded flower spikes. Feed in growing season.

❈❈❈ ☼–☼ ◐

Acer palmatum

Japanese maples have finely divided, palm-like leaves. Foliage colour varies from green to yellow to purple, turning a stunning fiery red in autumn. Choose a small variety for a container.

Care: Prune lightly in late winter for shape. Feed/water in growing season.

❈❈❈ ☼–☼ ◐

Fothergilla major

Easy-to-grow shrub with glossy, oval leaves that turn brilliant orange and crimson in autumn. Small, white, fragrant flowers in early spring. Brings charm and interest all the year round.

Care: Lightly prune for shape in late winter/early spring. Do not prune hard.

❈❈❈ ☼–☼ ◐

Canna

A tropical-style plant with large, upright leaves, often with striped markings or good color variations. Vibrant, showy flowers in late summer/early fall. Adds a dazzling late-season display.

Care: Leave to die back in fall. Protect over winter with mulch.

❈❈–❈ ☼ ◐

Fatsia japonica

Wonderful large, palmlike leaves that are glossy green all year round. A good architectural plant that needs a bit of space and can be underplanted with spring bulbs for seasonal color.

Care: Prune to shape in early spring. Water well in growing season.

❈❈❈ ☼–☼ ◐

Euonymous

Dwarf shrub with evergreen foliage, which is often variegated yellow or creamy white with green. Good for planting under large shrubs/trees or for brightening darker corners.

Care: Prune to shape in early spring. Water well in growing season.

❈❈❈ ☼–☼ ◐

See also... *Bergenia* p.227, *Buxus sempervirens* p.233, *Ferns* p.227, *Helleborus* p.227, *Hosta* p.227, *Photinia* p.229, *Pulmonaria* p.227, *Taxus baccata* p.229

Water and bog plants

Key to symbols: ◊ Drought tolerant ◐ Water often ● Keep constantly wet ☼ Grow in full sun ☼ Partial shade ☀ Full shade

Eichhornia crassipes

Water hyacinth has floating leaf stems to keep it on the surface. Delicate pale violet flowers in summer. Keep growth in check for small water features.

Care: Invasive. Remove plantlets regularly to reduce spreading. Do not put in natural water sources.

❄ ☼ ●

Nymphaea

Water lilies have showy, bowl-shaped flowers that come in various colors. Floating rounded leaves create shade for submerged water plants.

Care: Deadhead flowers and remove old foliage regularly. Feed in growing season with aquatic fertilizer.

❄❄❄ ☼ ●

Iris versicolor

Upright, swordlike leaves from early spring to late fall, with pretty blue and purple flowers in summer. Great for pond margins or boggy water features. Flowers are loved by insects.

Care: Remove dead foliage in late winter before new growth begins.

❄❄❄ ☼ ●

Caltha palustris

Bright and cheery in early spring, the marsh marigold has clusters of deep-yellow flowers and heart-shaped leaves from spring to fall. A natural plant choice for marsh or bog gardens.

Care: Cut back after flowering. Remove dead foliage in winter.

❄❄❄ ☼ ●

Zantedeschia aethiopica

Elegant white or yellow funnel-shaped flowers in spring and summer. Dark-green arrow-shaped leaves add interest from spring to fall.

Care: Remove dead foliage in late winter before new growth begins. May need protection from harsh winters.

❄❄–❄ ☼ ●

Carex elata

This evergreen sedge is perfect for the edge of marsh or bog gardens. Leaves are upright and yellow, with small black flowers in summer. Adds interest all year round.

Care: Cut back stalks after flowering and remove any dead foliage regularly.

❄❄❄ ☼–☼ ●

Plants for year-round interest

❋❋❋ Fully hardy ❋❋ Can survive outside in mild regions/sheltered sites ❋ Move inside for winter

Cornus

Dogwood has attractive colored stems from mid-green, orange, and red to purple-black. Foliage is green or variegated white. White flowers in summer; berries in fall.

Care: Hard prune every other year in late winter to 2–3in (5–7.5cm) above soil.

❋❋❋ ☼–◐ ◐

Hydrangea

For blue-flowered hydrangeas, plant in acidic soil. Pink ones prefer ordinary or alkaline soil. White-flowered species prefer some shade.

Care: Leave flower heads till late winter. Hard prune *H. arborescens* and *H. paniculata* to 2–3in (5–7.5cm) above soil.

❋❋❋ ◐ ◐

Calamagrostis x acutiflora
'Karl Foerster'

Ornamental grass with feathery flowers in late summer. The green foliage turns bronze in late summer, then provides interest during winter. Loved by birds.

Care: Leave stems and flowers over winter. Cut down in late winter.

❋❋❋ ☼–◐ ◐

Viburnum x bodnantense

Upright shrub with deciduous textured leaves. From fall to spring, clusters of scented, light-pink and white flowers bring winter color. Keep shrub height under control by pruning.

Care: Prune in late winter. Can be hard pruned if required.

❋❋❋ ☼–◐ ◐

Pyracantha

Evergreen shrub that can be grown as hedge or trained as specimens. Creamy white flowers in summer; long-lasting red/orange berries in fall. Loved by bees and birds.

Care: Prune to shape in early spring. Trim more often if used for hedging.

❋❋❋ ☼–◐ ◐

Buxus sempervirens

Evergreen boxwood is versatile. It can be clipped as a hedge or into topiary for extra interest. Slow-growing. Only needs 1–2 cuts a year to keep its shape.

Care: Prune to keep shape in early spring, just before growth starts. Water well in growing season.

❋❋❋ ☼ ◐ ◐

See also... *Carex elata* p.232, *Dipsacus fullonum* p.230, *Fothergilla major* p.231, *Heuchera* p.231, *Miscanthus sinensis* p.229, *Photinia* p.229, *Phyllostachys nigra* p.229, *Rosa rugosa* p.229, *Sedum* p.226

Get the Look

English garden

A mix of traditional flowering plants mingled with vegetables, fruit, and herbs makes for a gentle, romantic English garden look. Flowering plants are placed together in informal groups with different heights, shapes, and textures, creating a tapestry-style effect. Plants are left to self-seed to soften the edges of gravel or natural paving paths.

Plants to try

Alchemilla mollis	Fuchsias
Aster x frikartii 'Mönch'	Iris 'Jane Phillips'
Auriculas	Paeonia 'Sarah Bernhardt'
Campanula lactiflora	Primroses
Dianthus 'Mrs Sinkins'	Rosa 'William Lobb'
Dicentra spectablilis	Soft fruit and tree fruit
Digitalis purpurea	Sweet Peas
English Lavender	Viola odorata
	Wallflowers

Contemporary

Bold containers, formal lines, and architectural plants sum up the contemporary planting style. Use industrial materials for hard landscaping features —scaffolding boards for terraces, stainless steel for containers and raised beds, fences painted in bold colors. Add lighting to show off your garden area at night and to highlight specimen trees and shrubs.

Plants to try

Achillea 'Terracotta'
Buxus sempervirens
Cercidiphyllum japonicum
Colocasia esculenta
Fatsia japonica
Iris 'Jane Phillips'
Matteuccia struthiopteris
Phormium tenax
Phyllostachys nigra
Stipa gigantea
Succulents e.g., echeveria

YEAR-ROUND STYLE
Focal plants with strong outlines help to define the area all year round. Combine plants that flower at different times for successional interest.

Natural

Seek inspiration from the countryside, whether a wildflower meadow or a prairie. Use ornamental grasses to soften the look and emulate planting in natural habitats. This style is informal, colorful, relaxed, and spontaneous. Leave seedheads on over winter since these add further interest and structure.

Eryngium alpinum 'Superbum'

Knautia macedonica

Plants to try

Agastache 'Black Adder'
Calamagrostis x acutiflora
  'Karl Foerster'
Echinacea purpurea
  'Ruby Giant'
Eryngium alpinum
Gaura lindheimeri
Knautia macedonica

Molinia caerulea
Phlomis russelliana
Rudbeckia fulgida
  'Goldsturm'
Salvia x sylvestris
  'Mainacht'
Stipa gigantea
Stipa tennuissima
Verbena bonariensis

Mixed planting

Combining perennials with shrubs and trees will achieve a mixed planting style. Larger plants become focal points, while layers of perennials and bulbs add seasonal highlights. The style can be adapted for smaller spaces by choosing key structural plants and adding others in groups for a pleasing effect.

Plants to try

Allium 'Purple Sensation'
Artemisia 'Powis Castle'
Cornus alba 'Sibirica'
Cotinus coggygria
  'Royal Purple'
Geranium x 'Rozanne'
Hebe 'Red Edge'
Heuchera 'Plum Pudding'
Mahonia aquifolium
Papaver orientale
  'Perry's White'
Penstemon 'Hidcote Pink'
Perovskia 'Blue Spire'
Philadelphus 'Belle Etoile'
Rosa 'Iceberg'
Sedum 'Autumn Joy'

KEEP IT SIMPLE

Keep things simple and don't place too many different plants together since this will create a congested and complicated effect.

Small Space, Big Harvest

Think big, think creatively, and think bountiful. Your growing space may be tiny, but that doesn't mean your harvest needs to be small as well. By matching the right plants with the right growing conditions, you'll enjoy a delicious crop.

Growing plants for an edible crop is easy. Some plants may require a bit more attention than others, but don't be put off trying something new and different. Before you start growing, do some preparation and decide what you want to grow and how you are going to do it. Consider your space, too, and how it can be maximized: can you put pots and containers onto paved areas and steps? Can you hang planters from railings or use a vertical space to grow plants up and down? Try planting bush tomatoes or strawberries in hanging baskets, herbs in windowboxes, mini vegetables in patio containers, squashes and beans climbing up homemade tepee structures, lettuce in a kitchen colander. Be inspired by our projects, and try them out.

Fruit and vegetable know-how
With a little careful planning, and by selecting plants that are reliable, don't take up too much room, or can be grown in a different way, you'll get the most out of your space, whatever its size.

Dwarf varieties are versions of plants that have been bred to be smaller, but still produce a good and tasty yield. Dwarf runner, green, and broad beans don't need support or a frame to climb, and small carrots can easily be grown in containers, while dwarf plums, apples, peaches, and other fruit take up less space than their full-size relatives. Mini vegetables are either bred to be tiny, full-sized varieties that are picked when the crop is young, or plants grown close together, which will produce smaller and tastier crops. Micro gardening is growing plants in a tiny space or container. Choose some of the mini or

Luscious blueberries and strawberries are just some of the fruit that are easy to grow in containers.

dwarf varieties, or, if your container is really small, you can even enjoy tasty salad leaves from sprouting seeds in a cup.

Fast-growing edibles can be sown or planted in between slower-growing types as a catch crop. Summer salad plants, like lettuce, endive, radishes, beets, and green onions, are quick growers, as are spinach and bok choy. Try pea and bean shoots, too.

Training fruit makes good use of a compact growing space since it will help to maximize yields and looks very decorative. Apples, pears, cherries, currants, figs, and peaches can all be trained vertically as espaliers, cordons, standards, or fans against a fence or wall.

Mixing edibles and ornamentals will create a garden area that is pretty, productive, and like a mini kitchen garden. Some flowering plants act as natural disease repellents—planting marigolds, with their strong scent, next to tomatoes will help to keep bugs away, for example. Add decorative features, like homemade tepees for beans and peas, or use recycled containers for your plants. Consider how your plot will look as well as what is going in it.

Essential growing tips

Water well, and often Edible crops grown in containers need lots of water, sometimes twice a day in hot, dry weather. Give containers a thorough soaking—don't just water the top section of the pot. Adding a drip tray underneath is helpful so that the plant can take up water from the roots as well.

Protect Plants grown on balconies and high spaces will be more exposed to wind, rain, and sun than those grown at ground level. Foliage and soil mix will dry out more quickly in these conditions, so keep plants sheltered by adding screening.

Feed For a plant to produce a bountiful crop, you need to fertilize it first. Without the right nutrients, plants won't perform well and your crop will be small. Use diluted liquid feed when watering in the growing season, while diluted tomato fertilizer is great for other plants besides tomatoes and helps to boost crop production. Mix slow-release general fertilizer granules into the soil for extra nourishment. Wear gloves when handling all fertilizers.

Drainage Make sure all your containers have drainage holes for excess water to escape, otherwise roots will rot. Add a layer of drainage material, like gravel, small pebbles, or broken terra-cotta pots (crocks), at the bottom of containers before planting.

Crop rotation Don't plant the same vegetable in the same container year after year, unless you have changed the soil, since soil-borne diseases will build up and affect the plant's health and the quality of the crop. Rotate vegetables where you can.

Disguise functional containers and growing bags with a decorative covering, and group planters together for an ornamental effect

Fertilize and look after your edibles and they will reward you with a bountiful crop.

Summer vegetables

Key to symbols: ◌ Drought tolerant ◑ Water often ● Keep constantly wet ☼ Grow in full sun ☼ Partial shade ☀ Full shade

Eggplant

Perfect for containers. Mostly smooth, long, and slender with dark purple skin, but can also be round or pear-shaped, and white, pale lilac, streaked, or red.

Care: Keep in a sheltered, sunny location, well watered, and with high humidity. Mulch when in containers.

Lettuce

Lots of different types to choose from, with different shapes, textures, and colors. Cut-and-come-again lettuce is perfect for smaller containers.

Care: Sow in succession from spring to fall; some varieties can be overwintered. Don't let soil dry out.

Beets

Mostly round and purple, but can also be oval or long and bright red, golden yellow, and striped. Best eaten when young and sweet; leaves are also tasty.

Care: Sow successively for continuous supply throughout summer. Harvest remaining plants before frost.

Arugula

Peppery and spicy, arugula is easy to grow and tasty in salads. Wild arugula has narrower leaves than milder tasting salad arugula. Plants can be kept through the winter.

Care: Pick a few leaves at a time or cut the whole plant back to allow regrowth.

Cucumbers

Outdoor varieties are usually shorter than those grown under cover. Small, round cucumbers are sweet and tasty. Gherkins are preserved in vinegar or brined with herbs and spices.

Care: Grow up a tepee. Plants prefer lots of well-rotted organic matter in soil.

Tomatoes

Vine tomatoes have a tall central stem that needs support. Bush types are smaller and may not need support; some can be grown in hanging baskets. Fruit can be red, orange, or yellow.

Care: Choose a sunny site. Bring green fruit inside to ripen in late fall.

Also try... Chicory, Chile Peppers, Cucamelon, Endive, Gherkin, Peppers, Radicchio, Radishes

Herbs

❄❄❄ Fully hardy, blossoms may need frost protection ❄❄ Can survive in mild regions/sheltered sites ❄ Protect from frost

Basil

Easy to grow in a sunny sheltered spot or on a windowsill. Large-leaved is perfect for pesto; smaller and purple-leaved types are ideal for garnish. Also grows well with tomatoes.

Care: Sow indoors, then place outside in pots when risk of frost is over.

❄ ☼ ◊

Coriander

Distinctive flavor. Can grow quite tall, but regular harvesting will keep plants in check. Leave some to flower and set seed—they can also be used in cooking.

Care: Sow seeds direct in growing position at intervals. Protect later crops from harsher weather.

❄❄ ☼ ◊

Fennel

A perennial. The whole plant is edible. Leaves and seeds have stronger aniseed flavor than the root. Tall and graceful. Blends well with ornamental plants.

Care: Cut back plants in fall or remove heads after flowering to prevent too much self-seeding.

❄❄❄ ☼ ◊

Mint

Comes in a multitude of interesting flavors, with apple mint recommended for mint jelly and sauce. Some have variegated leaves and look ornamental.

Care: Can be very invasive; grow separately in a pot, or plant in a pot within another arrangement.

❄❄❄ ☼–◐ ◊

Sage

Attractive, aromatic evergreen shrub. Looks good in a flower border as well as a herb area. Green, purple, and variegated varieties add further interest. Leaves suit a wide variety of dishes.

Care: Choose well-drained soil mix for containers. Harvest leaves all year round.

❄❄❄ ☼ ◊

Thyme

Pretty, low-growing plant—ornamental as well as edible. There are many different varieties and all have lovely flowers. Leaf stalks dry well for cooking.

Care: Choose a warm, dry, sunny site. Cut back hard after flowering to maintain shape.

❄❄❄ ☼ ◊

Also try... Aniseed, Chervil, Lovage, Oregano, Parsley, Sage, Sweet Marjoram, Tarragon

Essential Garden Tools

There are a few tools and materials you'll need to look after your plants and garden area. Make the tools part of your garden display by storing them in an attractive cupboard or use a small table that could also double as a plant display area, and hang smaller items from hooks on trellis.

Trowel
Essential for planting, scooping soil mix, and removing weeds.

Watering can
Use one with a detachable nozzle so that you can get the spout directly into pots and containers.

Hand fork
Useful to lightly dig in between plants and incorporate granular fertilizer.

Mini hoe
A useful tool to help with weeding between tightly packed plants.

Long-handled tools
These are perfect to use on larger containers and raised beds.

Pruners
Essential for pruning, cutting back plants, and harvesting.

Water mister
Great for spritzing moisture and humidity on to plants in warmer weather. Also good for liquid foliar fertilizer.

TOOL MAINTENANCE

It is worth taking the time to keep tools clean by removing soil and potting mix after use. At the end of the main gardening season, lightly oil metal surfaces to prevent any rust. If you look after your tools, they will last for years.

Tub
Very handy for collecting plant debris. Also useful for holding soil mix when planting, and for immersing plants for watering.

Garden fabric
Protects plants and seedlings from frost in winter and early spring.

Gloves
Choose reasonably tight-fitting, waterproof ones so you can still handle tools and plants.

Pots
Classic terra-cotta pots are attractive in themselves and can be customized with paint effects.

Crocks
Broken clay pots, used for drainage. Gravel and small pebbles can also be used.

Garden twine
For tying plants to structures as they grow and lots of other uses in the gardening space.

Drip tray
Put these under your containers so plants can take up water from their roots.

Kneeler
Choose a comfy one that will protect your knees when attending to low planting.

Bamboo poles
Available in lots of sizes, great for supporting plants and creating structures for climbers.

YOU MAY ALSO NEED

Plastic sheeting A plastic groundsheet is useful for spreading out to protect surfaces when you garden.

Garden wire Plastic-coated and stronger than twine, useful for weightier objects.

Netting To protect edibles from birds and insects.

Plant markers So you never forget what you've planted!

Caring for Your Plants

Spend just a little bit of time choosing the right potting mix and meeting the watering, feeding, and care requirements of your plants, and you will reap the rewards: healthy growth and a good, productive yield of flowers or crops.

Potting mix

Most plants will grow well in general multipurpose potting mix, but some have special requirements or are more suited to free-draining soil or acidic mix. You should always read plant labels for a guide to soil requirements, but it's also a good idea to do a bit of your own research before you plant anything, so that you can buy the correct potting mix.

Free-draining soil Generally, anything that likes a lot of sun, such as succulents and cacti, prefers a free-draining, gritty soil mix, so choose one with horticultural sand already mixed in, or add perlite, granules of volcanic minerals, or horticultural grit.

Acidic soil Blueberries, azaleas, rhododendrons, and heathers need acidic or ericaceous soil and will die if planted in multipurpose potting mix.

Seed potting mix This has no soil or nutrients and is also perfect for adult plants that require minimal nutrients, such as wildflowers.

Healthy additives

Incorporate well-rotted manure and/or homemade compost into your soil to help retain moisture, improve soil texture, and add plenty of healthy minerals. Mix into your soil or apply as mulch in spring. Not all plants need it, but edibles, shrubs, and trees will appreciate the boost. Whatever you use, make sure it is well-rotted because fresh compost produces too much heat as it decays; leave garden compost to rot for at least six months.

Watering

Containers tend to dry out more quickly than plants in the ground; those on balconies or exposed above ground level need particular attention. Make sure all your containers have drainage holes; if not, make them yourself using a drill or similar. If plants sit in too much water their roots will rot—unless they are bog or water plants, of course. Roots also need air

Home composting

Add fruit and vegetable peelings to an outside compost bin where you can also put prunings. Mix plant matter with plenty of shredded paper and cardboard, and turn everything regularly to keep the air circulating and to aid decay. Don't add woody stems, weeds, diseased plants, or meat, fish, or cooked food. Keep the bin covered, but be sure it isn't too dry, and add water if necessary. It should take six to nine months to rot down.

A covered pot in the kitchen is handy for storing fruit and vegetable peelings before transferring them to an outside compost bin.

circulation, so add crocks (broken terra-cotta pots) or gravel to the bottom of containers before adding soil mix. A drip tray underneath will protect surfaces from water and allow plants to soak up moisture via their roots. Plants that prefer moisture-retentive soil, such as ferns, still require drainage, but conserve moisture by mulching with organic material or sphagnum moss.

How and when to water

Water plants regularly and frequently. Plants will need more watering while they are establishing, and vegetables and fruit need plenty as flowers and crops form. In hot, dry conditions water containers twice a day. Fill the container to the rim, then let it drain and water again. Watering just a little doesn't get moisture to the roots. Check containers each day from mid-spring to early fall for moisture content. Some plants, like succulents or air plants, will not require watering daily, so check the plant's watering needs when you buy. You can give plants extra moisture by misting in hot weather. Make sure you water at the right time of day, too. Early morning or evening are best so that leaves aren't scorched by the sun and the water

doesn't evaporate as quickly. Water plants only during the growing season, as most plants don't need watering when dormant in winter and prefer slightly dry soil mix so their roots don't get wet or frozen.

Watering help

Mix water-storing crystals into potting mix at planting time. These expand to hold moisture and release it as the soil mix dries. Irrigation systems are also useful for larger areas or if you don't want to worry about watering every day. Many systems work on a timer and are great if you go away.

DIY Weekend Waterer Making your own simple irrigation system is easy. Drill a hole for a plastic tap near the bottom of a bucket. Attach a length of hose to the tap. Prick tiny holes in the hose and stop up the end. Place the bucket on a raised platform, then fill with water. Feed the hose over your plant pots and open the tap to let a small amount of water flow.

Watering requirements can vary dramatically depending on the plant. Some, such as air plants, are not watered at the roots at all; they are only watered by misting.

A simple weekend watering system is easy to make yourself and provides a gentle supply of water to your plants for several days.

Feeding

Plants, especially those in containers, need regular feeding in the growing season to keep them healthy and productive. Liquid fertilizer, such as kelp extract, is added to your watering can. You can also add diluted tomato feed to many ornamental and edible plants. Soluble granular fertilizers include fish, blood, and bone and general purpose; sprinkle into the potting mix at planting, or add around the plant base monthly. Ensure the granules do not touch plants. Wear gloves when handling fertilizers, and always check the manufacturer's instructions for dosage.

Only feed plants from spring to fall; most do not need it when dormant in winter. Some require little or no feeding. Do not overfertilize or you will have abundant foliage at the expense of flowers or crops.

FOLIAR FEED

Boost plants by misting diluted liquid fertilizer onto foliage to keep them lush and healthy. The feed is taken up through the leaves.

Dilute liquid fertilizer in your watering can.

Protect fruit bushes from birds using netting.

General care

Protect young plants and fruit blossoms from frost in early spring by covering with garden fabric. Close to harvest time, fruit plants can be protected from birds by netting. Protect plants in higher locations from wind damage by adding screening or choosing plants that can survive in exposed sites.

Keep plants looking healthy by removing any dead, diseased, or dying foliage regularly during the growing season. Don't compost diseased plant material since this could spread diseases to other plants. Some plants, such as succulents, need a good clean up of spent flower stalks and old leaves before they go dormant, otherwise this dead material may rot the plant. Others, like echinacea, have lovely seedheads that add winter interest and provide food for beneficial creatures, so don't cut these back until late winter or early spring.

Harvesting

Some fruit and vegetables need to mature fully before harvesting; others can be eaten while they are young and tasty. Apples, pears, strawberries, cauliflower, and broccoli, for example, need time to develop and don't taste good when unripe, but peas, zucchini, radishes, and beans are sweet and tasty when picked young and fresh. Many crops are best eaten right away, but if you need to store produce, choose a cool, dry, dark place; don't store bruised or damaged crops since they could encourage good crops to rot. Fruit such as apples and pears can be individually wrapped for storage, but check each one regularly for signs of decay and remove affected fruit. Many vegetables, herbs, and some soft fruit can be frozen, dried, or pickled—a lovely way to share your homegrown edibles with friends and family.

Homegrown seeds

Harvest seeds from flowers and vegetables at the end of their growing season. You may not get a pure offspring from the parent plant, depending on the variety and what was grown nearby, but it is fun to raise your own plants from homegrown seeds. Allow edible crops to fully ripen and flowers to set ripe seed before harvesting, and collect when the seed pod is dry. Use a paper or plastic bag to collect the seed, then store in an airtight container or paper bag until ready to sow. Depending on the plant, you can sow some seed right away. The germination rate will deteriorate over time, so try to use your gathered seed within a year for best results.

Easy-care edibles

Choose fruit and vegetable varieties that have been selected by growers as good-quality crops that can manage pests and resist disease. Some examples are lettuce, spinach, and beets that don't bolt; potatoes and tomatoes that are blight resistant; fruit grown on dwarf rooting stock; and crops resistant to mildew.

Above: Radishes can be harvested while small, young, and tasty.

Left: Pears need to fully mature before picking.

Garden Year Planner

Spring

PREPARATION
- Tidy up containers and planting areas, replacing or topping off soil if required.
- Sweep up leaves and debris. Wash down areas as needed.

GROW
- Sow seeds from early spring. Some need to be sown indoors for frost protection.
- Buy young plants. Those for summer bedding displays are not frost hardy so will need protection until the danger of frost is over.
- Begin to water and feed plants in containers, increasing frequency as the weather gets warmer.

PLANT CARE
- Cut back old and dead foliage from plants in early spring before new growth begins to emerge.

OTHER WORK
- Consider any new planting areas or ideas, and source plants.

Summer

PREPARATION
- Clean outdoor furniture.

GROW
- Continue sowing seeds of summer vegetables at regular intervals for successional crops.
- Tie in climbing plants to frames and check if other plants need support with sticks or a trellis.
- Water plants often in hot weather, when soil will dry out quickly.

PLANT CARE
- Deadhead flowers regularly on ornamental plants to encourage repeat flowering.
- Harvest crops when ripe.

OTHER WORK
- Consider watering requirements if you are going away on vacation.

Fall

PREPARATION
- Give containers a clean and check soil levels, topping with potting mix if required.
- Make sure all structures and climbing and larger plants are secure.

GROW
- Remove summer bedding plants and plant fall and winter plants as well as spring bulbs.
- Harvest edible crops and store excess produce. Remove plants after harvesting is finished.
- Start to reduce watering and feeding.

PLANT CARE
- Continue to deadhead flowers on ornamental plants to enjoy any late flowering displays.

OTHER WORK
- Keep walkways and terraces clear of leaves, twigs, and other debris.

To find out if seeds need to be sown indoors, check the information on the packet carefully.

Tie in climbing plants, such as honeysuckle, that need support during the growing season.

Some edible crops, like squash, store well in a cool, ventilated place.

Winter

PREPARATION
- Store or cover outdoor furniture.
- Wrap containers with fabric or bubble wrap if required.
- Move any frost-tender plants to a light, frost-free place.
- Check if containers are frost hardy.

GROW
- Do not water or feed dormant plants.
- Plant bare root, ornamental specimens if weather conditions are favorable and the soil is not frozen.

PLANT CARE
- Tidy up plants but leave some seedheads over winter for birds to enjoy and for ornamental interest.

OTHER WORK
- Order seed catalogs. Make notes of what you'd like to grow next year.
- Order and buy bare root plants.

For winter color, hellebores flower from midwinter to spring, depending on the species.

Garden Doctor

Maintaining a healthy, ecological balance and having a proactive approach helps with pest and disease control. Here are some simple and practical tips:

Look after your soil Add organic matter in spring; replace or renew potting mix in containers regularly.
Follow crop rotation Rotate edible crops to help reduce buildup of soilborne diseases.
Choose resistance Use certified virus-free or disease-resistant seeds and plants, especially for edible crops.
Be vigilant Examine plants regularly and treat any pests or diseases as soon as signs of damage appear.
Encourage nature's little helpers Grow plants that attract beneficial insects (see pages 210–15).

Companion planting

By growing certain plants near others you can help reduce pests and diseases. For example, the scent of French marigolds discourages whiteflies; basil can be planted with tomatoes to improve growth and flavor; and garlic planted near roses discourages greenflies.

A mixture of flowering plants and edible crops looks attractive and can deter pests and diseases.

Index

About the author

Based near Cambridge, UK, RHS medal award-winning garden designer and gardening journalist Philippa Pearson takes inspiration for her garden creations from the countryside, classical and contemporary architecture, and textiles. Her design portfolio covers many private gardens across the UK and her colorful planting style attracts much attention from visitors, the media, and photographers at RHS shows, and is greatly enjoyed by her garden design clients. Philippa enjoys the challenge of creating gardens in smaller spaces, as well as larger ones. www.philippapearson.co.uk

Acknowledgments

Author's acknowledgments
The author would like to thank the following for their help supplying plants, equipment, information, and proofreading: Fiona Wemyss from Blueleaf Plants; Jo Woffinden; Mark Smith from Key Essentials; Luci Skinner from Woottens Plants; Peter Warren, Bonsai professional; Mark Haslett from Essex Carnivorous Plants; Chris Crow from Sarracenia Nurseries; and everyone who lent us their garden or balcony for photos.

The author would also like to thank especially the wonderful team at DK who have supported and helped her: Alastair Laing, Sonia Moore, Vicky Read, Holly Kyte, Penny Warren, Mary Ling, and Jane Bull.

Publisher's acknowledgments
DK would like to thank:

Katie Federico for project assistance; Geremia Federico for project consultancy and carpentry; Scott Flashman for design and carpentry on the hanging plant pot mobile; Peter Warren for his bonsai expertise, www.saruyama.co.uk.

The following people and organisations for generously allowing us to create projects and photograph in their garden spaces: Laura and Ed Buller, Satu Fox, Guy and Juliette Harvey, Rosemary Hignett, Hoa Luc, Sonia Moore, Philippa Pearson, Ron and Rita Saunders, Vauxhall City Farm, Chris Roos and Amy Wagner, Fiona Wemyss, Hin-Yan Wong.

Hand models: Katie Federico, Satu Fox, Alastair Laing, Max Moore, Harriet Stanton, Ciaran Webster, Fiona Wemyss.

Paula Johnson and the staff at Squires Garden Centre, Stanmore; Jacques Amand International Ltd, Stanmore, for plants and advice; Garden Brocante, Shiplake, for supplying galvanized metal planters; The Boma Garden Centre, Kentish Town; Tim Bailey at the Carnivorous Plants Society, for cultivation advice, www.thecps.org.uk; Alex Roberts at Chive.

Marie Lorimer for indexing.

Laura Nickoll for proofreading.

Nidhi Mathur for editorial assistance.

Picture credits
The publisher would like to thank the following for their kind permission to reproduce their photographs:

(Key: a-above; b-below/bottom; c-centre; f-far; l-left; r-right; t-top)

225 Dorling Kindersley: Designed by Nilufer Danis / RHS Hampton Court Flower Show 2012 (t). **230 Dorling Kindersley:** RHS Garden, Wisley (cla). **236 Dorling Kindersley:** Alan Buckingham (cr, fcr). **237 Dorling Kindersley:** Designed by Heather Culpan and Nicola Reed (bl). **239 Dorling Kindersley:** Designed by Linda Fairman of Oasthouse Nursery / RHS Hampton Court Flower Show 2012 (ca). **242 Dorling Kindersley:** Alan Buckingham (ca, cra, clb, cb, crb). **243 Dorling Kindersley:** Linda Fairman of Oasthouse Nursery / RHS Hampton Court Flower Show 2012 (cra).

All other images © Dorling Kindersley
For further information see:
www.dkimages.com